WALLACE-HOMESTEAD PRICE GUIDE TO

AMERICAN *COUNTRY* ANTIQUES

NINTH EDITION

DON AND CAROL RAYCRAFT

Wallace-Homestead Book Company

Radnor, Pennsylvania

Library of Congress Catalog Card Number 86–640023
ISBN 0–87069–524–x

Designed by Anthony Jacobson
Manufactured in the United States of America
Cover photo by Carol Raycraft

 2 3 4 5 6 7 8 9 0   8 7 6 5 4 3 2 1 0

CONTENTS

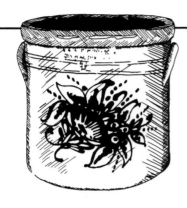

3 Decorated Stoneware & Yellowware 76

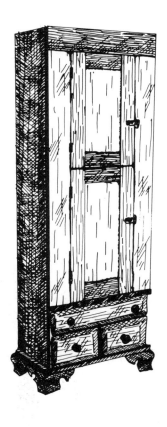

ACKNOWLEDGMENTS

Linda Moor Anelli
The Antique Mall of Chenoa
Al Behr
Roy and Pat Buncher
Mary Burgess
Lezlie Colburn
Copake Country Auctions
David Debandi
Byron and Sara Dillow
Hannah Elizabeth Doak
Martha Doak
Richard I. Doak Jr.
Teri and Joe Dziadul
Michael Fallon
Patrick and Chris Francomano
Frank's Antiques, Hillard, Florida
Bernie Green
Howie and Iris Hirsch

Ann and Tom Hixson
Rose Holtzclaw
General Alex Hood (retired)
Judy Judd
Lancaster Antique Market
Barry and Lisa McAllister
Marie and David Oldread
Peoria Antiques Center
Joe and Opal Pickens
Father Tom Pincelli
John and Mary Purvis
Steve Rhodes
Kevin and Debbie Shimansky
Ellen Tatem
Dr. J.B. Wells
Jim White
Eve Wilson
Mr. and Mrs. Richard Zanetti

PHOTOGRAPHY

Al Behr
Joe Dziadul
Ann Hixson
Lisa McAllister
John Purvis
Carol Raycraft
R. Craig Raycraft
Ellen Tatem
Richard Zanetti

WALLACE-HOMESTEAD
PRICE GUIDE TO

AMERICAN
COUNTRY
ANTIQUES

INTRODUCTION

Wallace Nutting's *Furniture of the Pilgrim Century* was published in 1924. The book contains more than 1500 photographs of seventeenth- and eighteenth-century American furniture that most of us will never see for sale, cannot afford, and have no place to put anyway. Nutting's massive work gave wealthy collectors of 75 years ago an appreciation of what was available.

Nutting's book also included a small section of advice to potential collectors about how to find antiques. He suggested that it would be a good idea for collectors to take pictures of desired items to "small" dealers and ask them to be on the watch for the desired items as they make their rounds. He didn't advocate knocking on doors, but he mentioned that it would be wise for the collector to take another photograph along to show the householder what piece the collector was trying to find.

Nutting did make several valuable points that have transcended the years and have merit for us today. Many dealers know that specific collectors are looking for particular pieces and will pay for the opportunity to own them. For example, a dealer from Iowa may be on a buying trip in New Hampshire and see a painted Shaker box. The dealer may have only one client who has ever expressed an interest in such a box. The dealer would normally not buy the box because it is expensive and she has "nowhere to go with it." The only way the box could "have anything left in it" for her is for her to telephone the collector in Iowa, describe the box in detail, offer a price, and get a yes answer. Normally on transactions like this there are no returns. The customer must have enough faith in the dealer to purchase the item without seeing it.

Nutting also stated that many times when a collector stumbles over a piece in the home of an owner the price asked by the owner is much higher than the asking price would be if the item were in an antiques shop. The owner has little idea as to the actual value of the item and pulls a price out of the air.

Nutting also pointed out in 1924 that "the gullible are being taken in every day by spurious articles or by extreme prices." They still are.

Collecting

There is a natural progression through which most country antiques collectors pass. Perhaps you are given an oak table or chair by a relative. One piece of oak gradually leads to a roomfull. Most of the pieces are heavily refinished, much loved, and highly polished. You then add a few molded stoneware crocks with stenciled decorations to several factory-made baskets to create a room setting.

A chance visit to an antiques shop or a home filled with painted furniture and "bird"-decorated stoneware plants a seed that eventually grows into a gradual disenchantment with oak and other mass-produced "antiques." Then comes a burning desire to replicate rooms shown in *Country Living* and *Country Home* in your own home, and the hunt begins. That hunt usually continues until the family gathers and the doctor pulls the sheet over your head.

We were fortunate enough to bypass several of these steps when we began to collect American antiques in the mid-1960s, because we came under the influence of a middle-aged couple who had already been down that road. They helped us with valuable insights about things to buy, pieces to avoid, and places to go. They also told us what to do after we got to those places.

When we started looking for books about antiques, we found few available that contained information relevant to our collecting needs. There were important books about the Pilgrim Century furniture (furniture we could not locate or afford) but little about what we liked. Eventually we began to write the kind of books we couldn't find for people who had similar interests.

The Capricious Market

Some theorists feel that the antiques market and prices can be manipulated. An article in *Country Living* several years ago included numerous birdhouses of varying quality. That article set off a mania among the readers to secure as many birdhouses as possible to duplicate the look. Plywood birdhouses from the 1950s suddenly were being cut out of trees and piled in the rear of Volvo station wagons for the trip back to the suburbs.

One of the more bizzare happenings in the collectibles area occurred in May of 1988 with the sale of Andy Warhol's estate in New York City. Among his hundreds of collections, Warhol had accumulated 155 ceramic cookie jars that dated from the 1940s through the 1960s. The presale estimate for the jars was $150 to $200 for a lot of four. The same cookie jars could probably be purchased every Sunday at local flea markets for $15 to $40. The inflated estimate was due to Warhol's ownership and the public's desire to buy something from his collection that could be purchased inexpensively.

The first lot sold for $1980, and people were stunned. Several were probably speechless later when two cookie jars and a pair of salt and pepper shakers brought $23,100. The total selling price of the 155 cookie jars at auction was $247,830.

A single individual captured 33 of the 38 lots of jars for a total of $198,605. The man could have taken a week off and visited shops, flea markets, and antiques malls in New York and Pennsylvania and found a comparable collection of 155 cookie jars for a total of $3000 to $5000 plus gas, Pepsi, pizzas, and Howard Johnson's, but the jars wouldn't have been owned by Andy Warhol.

Clearly, the provenance of the jars was what people were buying. The incredible selling prices will have little long-term effect on the price of cookie jars. A cookie jar is still just a cookie jar, unless it was owned by Andy Warhol.

We have always taken the approach that you buy something because you think it's great and have a place to put it so you can enjoy it. We have never bought cupboards or butter molds because we thought they would increase dramatically in price and become exceptional investments. We have been concerned only with authenticity, original paint or finish, degree of rarity, price, and whether or not we had a place to put an item so we could see it every day. Twenty years ago we had numerous opportunities to buy great Midwestern quilts at what would now be considered bargain prices. We bought a few over the years but never really took the time to understand or appreciate them until it was too late and supplies had diminished and prices skyrocketed.

"Country is Dead"

Several years ago we traveled to Pennsylvania to speak to a group of collectors who had driven from a 100-mile radius to hear about American country antiques at a one-day seminar. The sponsor of the event was a nationally known antiques author and columnist who was slated to share the speaking assignment with us. All of the people who showed up that day were obviously interested in country antiques, or they wouldn't have paid the seminar fee for a light lunch and six hours of slides and discussion.

The host gave us a lengthy and cordial introduction and concluded by saying, "Country is dead." The members of the audience were somewhat taken aback by his negative prognostication because they had paid their money and were getting ready to learn as much about country as they possibly could during the seminar.

The idea that "country is dead" is important only to individuals who are concerned with the style or "look" of the moment, as dictated by the home furnishing magazines. Several years ago, quilts in pastel colors were plentiful and inexpensive. An article or two that declared pastels as the major country colors caused the prices to jump threefold in a short time period. Individuals who wanted their furnishings to be stylish immediately purchased whatever pastels they could find.

The "country look" has a tendency to change or be modified constantly. Businesses and magazines want to sell their product. If there is not constant change in "fashionable" color, fabric, and style, businesses and magazines won't make any money because people will be content with what they have and stay away from the marketplace.

The October 20, 1988, edition of *USA Today* pointed out another change in the direction of the country look. One designer was quoted as saying: "We're a little tired of American country. We've had it a long time, and it's a little cluttered. We were looking for another look."

Scandinavian country, a recent fashionable look, highlights pastel colors, floral motifs, and ribbons and bows. Prices on new pieces range from $1100 for a three-drawer chest from Thomasville to $3000 for a hand-painted cupboard from Jeffco. Our experience has been that a piece of new furniture, like a new automobile, does not hold its value very well. This may be due in part to the availability of duplicate pieces. If the people across the street want a piece just like yours, they can go to the furniture dealer and write a check. The next evolution of the fashionable look may go from Scandinavian country to something else, and the proud owner of Scandinavian pieces is left with yesterday's furniture with a severely deflated value. On the other hand, a collector of country antiques can still find an exceptional "hand-painted" nineteenth-century cupboard for less than $3000 that will provide aesthetic enjoyment and serious investment potential for the long term.

There is no doubt that individuals who have purchased contemporary country crafts and furnished their homes with Styrofoam watermelons, plywood birdhouses, and wreaths made of plastic bread wrappers eventually will move on to the next style of the moment, and for them country *will* be dead. Those of us who have driven hundreds of miles for pine cupboards that were already sold, hit our heads on low beams in damp basements, and eaten week-old ham salad in a small town in the middle of a Kansas wheat field will keep what we have and pass it on to our children to cherish as much as we have.

1

BUYING COUNTRY ANTIQUES

Urban Antiques Shows

Dealers who take part in large urban antiques shows typically have considerable expenses that must be passed on to the consumer. Rental space at a nationally advertised New York City show may be several thousands of dollars. Other costs include travel, lodging, food, parking, taxicabs, porters, and tips. To have a successful show, dealers must sell a great deal of merchandise. It makes no sense to fill a booth with $125 stoneware crocks or $28 butter paddles. Dealers must have high-ticket items that generate significant dollars. Collectors with extensive budgets can find truly great pieces of Americana at many of the "prestige" shows and enjoy champagne and a gourmet buffet. (At a fall 1988 show in New York City, collectors attending a catered preview paid $750 for the privilege of dining and shopping early.) Bargains at a show of this type may be harder to find than a lemonade shake-up and a corn dog.

The dealers who do these shows tend to specialize in a particular period of furniture or type of antique. Few "general line" dealers—who sell combinations of jewelry, quilts, baskets and Depression glass—get in the door. Because of dealer specialization, most dealers at the "prestige" shows are well informed about their merchandise and price their items accordingly. Seldom does an unusual antique go unrecognized and appear in a booth underpriced.

Antiques Shops

If you are driving from shop to shop in a specific geographic area, it is a wise move to obtain a free map from a local dealers association that lists all the member shops and the range of items each one sells. The maps can be picked up in the shops of member dealers. Most of the dealers associations also sponsor antiques shows once or twice a year.

There are also numerous guides that are available in paperback form that show where the antiques shops are located within a two- or three-state area. Do not assume that every shop in the area is in the guide, because the guide is done by subscription.

The dealer pays the publisher for the right to be included, and many shops may choose not to participate. It is important to ask at each shop if there are other dealers in the immediate area who carry the kind of merchandise you are seeking.

Antiques shops do not have to be on major highways or in large cities to be successful. If the merchandise is of high quality and in an attractive setting, collectors will drive almost anywhere to buy. It is always a wise move to call ahead and make an appointment at a shop rather than driving 50 miles only to find the door locked and a rapid dog overseeing the premises.

Flea Markets

Flea markets are held within 50 miles of almost any town in America every weekend. The majority are not worth the effort required to fight the heat, dust, crowds, and food that routinely defies description. The quality of merchandise typically ranges from tube sox to tube sox with stripes.

A flea market can be a huge fairgrounds with metal buildings that hold three hundred 4' × 6' booths and 5' aisles that allow you to get locked between two people you would normally cross a four-lane expressway at rush hour to avoid. The buildings are typically surrounded by a 50-acre field that is a dust bowl in August and a bottomless bog in April. The field is filled with dealers who *want to sell* their merchandise. They have not come to the flea market because it will add to their prestige

and bring additional business to their antiques shops. Most flea market dealers sell only at the flea market. Their inventory is not purchased at urban auctions or suburban antiques shows. Most find their goods at farm auctions, junk shops, house calls, backyard estate auctions, and other flea markets. Local garage sales also occasionally turn up an underpriced item that can be turned for a profit at the flea market. Few flea market dealers spend significant time reworking, repairing, or refinishing furniture. They buy it and attempt to sell it quickly.

STRATEGY

It is possible to find a major piece of furniture at a flea market if you are in the right place at the golden moment when a great piece comes off the truck or appears from under a $75 Sears, Roebuck & Company veneered oak desk.

To be in the right place requires considerable thought and effort. It is critical to get into the flea market at the time the dealers are setting up to get the best shot at what is available. There are a variety of dubious techniques that can be used to get into the flea market during the setup period. They range from carrying a box of "antiques" through the door for a mythical dealer's booth to begging the security guard at the main gate. The most successful and least threatening is to volunteer your efforts to a local dealer to assist in the unpacking and loading process.

Some flea market operators allow customers to buy an inflated "early bird" ticket that provides admission an hour or two before the gates are opened. This gives the serious consumer a chance to buy before the rest of the civilians are allowed to enter.

Many times dealers sell more to each other wholesale, prior to the flea market's opening, than they do retail to the general public during the show. If you buy your ticket an hour after the gate is opened, the odds of finding a great underpriced piece are slim. Bargains that do turn up after the setup period is completed probably have slipped through because they are too esoteric for nonexperts to recognize. A great pie safe or cupboard that is marked $250 will probably be purchased off the truck during the unloading process; however, a one-of-a-kind pocket tobacco tin that few people have seen before may still be on a table for $16.50 twenty minutes before the flea market closes.

Size. Flea markets are found in a variety of sizes almost everywhere. They range from parking lot markets with 15 to 20 dealers to huge markets that contain more than 1500 dealers and 20,000 customers.

Nonselectivity. Among many serious antiques collectors, flea markets tend to have a negative connotation. A flea market dealer may offer for sale almost any items that may be legally sold within the specific geographic area. Flea market promoters are seldom selective in their choices of dealers who are allowed to participate. If a dealer can write a "good" check or has the booth rent in cash, that dealer usually has a spot. Promoters like to advertise the quantity of dealers rather than the quality of the goods for sale.

Admission. Most flea markets have specific hours over a single day or weekend and charge admission (usually $1–$3). Dealers rent specific sizes of indoor or outdoor booths and offer their wares. Indoor booths typically are at least 50 percent more expensive to rent than outdoor booths.

Prices. Prices are usually much more negotiable at a flea market than at a conventional antiques show or antiques market. The flea market dealer's primary mission is to sell. As the day goes on, prices have been known to evaporate a bit. A 7' corner cupboard is especially susceptible to the heat and the potential of having to be repacked on the truck for the long ride home. It is possible that the price may drop 30 to 40 percent in the last hours of the market.

Effort. Generally there is such a huge assortment of trash, crafts, car parts, month-old donuts, flowers, clothing, and ephemera that it takes hours to sift through it to find any antiques items of quality. Many antiques collectors are not conditioned to that type of activity. They like to look leisurely through room-setting booths in 72° comfort and buy from dealers who don't look like they fell off a rutabaga truck on the way into town.

Bargains. The absolutely best aspect of most flea markets is the uncertainty of what you are going to find. There is still a thrill of anticipation for us even after 25 years of attending markets across the country. Once or twice a year we find something that wipes out the memory of being shut out on a 98° day in July. The key to success at any flea market is to get inside the doors during the setup period or as quickly as possible after the doors open. The alternative approach to finding a bargain is to wait until the last hours of the flea market and purchase a large piece of furniture from a small dealer with a bad back and nobody to help load it on the truck.

Antiques Markets

Antiques markets are very attractive to dealers because they provide the potential for large crowds with a minimal investment in time and overhead expenses. There are primarily two distinct types of antiques markets in operation, multiple shows and one-time (annual) shows. Many markets are held six, eight, or twelve times a year on a regular date (for example, the third Sunday or first weekend of the month) at a fairgrounds or facility with extensive parking and buildings for inside dealers. Typically, these markets are near a populated area with nearby interstate highways. These markets are often heavily advertised and bring dealers from several states. The alternative to multiple shows or markets is the prestigous one- or two-day show often held annually to benefit a local charity or historical site.

The Shaker Museum Show near Chatham, New York, in early August is a one-day outdoor event that annually draws some of the nation's premier dealers in New England and American country antiques. The area has a number of wealthy collectors with summer homes who annually look forward to the show. A dealer can sell thousands of dollars worth of merchandise and have only the expenses of space rental, gas, and lunch. A show like this is very selective about the dealers it allows to exhibit. It may take years for a dealer to get into the show, even if the dealer has high-quality American antiques.

Antiques markets differ from flea markets in their level of selectivity. The promoters of antiques markets usually want a great many dealers, but they want those dealers to sell only antiques or collectibles. New merchandise is usually prohibited.

The line that separates collectibles and antiques tends to get thinner every year. Most antiques markets allow collectible dealers to participate. A collectible is an item that was produced in moderate to large quantities and was not considered especially important at the time it was manufactured. Baseball cards, Elvis Presley memorabilia, postcards, World War II uniforms, Avon bottles, beer cans, and Shirley Temple paper dolls are some of the numerous items that turn up in the booths of dealers who specialize in collectibles.

One of the nation's finest outdoor antiques markets is held in early September each year in Farmington, Connecticut. More than 600 dealers converge on the Polo Grounds in Farmington for the annual event. The first Farmington show was held in 1980 and has grown every year. The show usually runs from 10 a.m. until 6 p.m. on Saturday and 9 a.m. to 4 p.m. on Sunday.

Collectors have the opportunity to pay $10 on Saturday for an early bird admission, which allows them to shop from 7:30 a.m. A $10 early bird ticket is probably a good investment at a market or show the quality of Farmington, since it gives the purchaser a 2½-hour head start over people who choose to wait and purchase a general admission ticket. It is important to note that even with an early bird ticket most of the participating dealers have "picked" or shopped the show to some extent during the setup period. When the general admission people troop in at the opening, two distinct groups of serious buyers—dealers and "early birds"—have already made their rounds. Some show promoters attempt to restrict transactions among dealers before the start of a show, but this practice is extremely difficult to monitor.

In August of 1988 we attended the 3rd Sunday Market in Bloomington, Illinois, and watched an open cupboard sell three times in a period of one hour before the show opened. The softwood cupboard was in "as found" condition and had a worn finish, but it was structurally sound and dated from about the middle of the nineteenth century. The cupboard had come out of a farm sale in southern Illinois a few days before and was offered for $550 at the market. It quickly sold and was resold for $750 about 20 minutes later. Shortly before the market opened for business on Sunday morning, the cupboard was purchased for $1250. The three brief owners of the cupboard bought it wholesale and sold it wholesale before it was ever offered to a retail customer.

This farm cupboard example illustrates the importance of attempting to secure early entry into a show. For $40 a collector and a friend could have bought an early bird admission into the 3rd Sunday Market on Saturday while the dealers were unloading and putting their booths together. If a collector is serious about purchasing antiques, it makes a great deal of sense to have the opportunity to see the merchandise as "early" as possible.

- Dealers like antiques markets because they normally have moderate booth rents, large crowds, low overhead, and an easy setup.
- For an antiques market to be successful, the promoters of the market must find a location that is accessible, contains ample parking, and has a population base to provide a crowd.
- The antiques market does not have to be in an urban setting, but it should be able to draw from one within a 30- to 40-mile radius.
- Antiques markets occasionally specialize in a particular period of merchandise. A market in Connecticut could be limited to only dealers in New England and American country antiques and be successful with large crowds of buyers. However, an antiques market in North Dakota or Florida that specialized in Americana would not find enough dealers or customers to generate a successful operation.
- For an antiques market to be profitable for the promoters and dealers there must be an abundance of advertising and quality control. New merchandise should not be allowed, or else what was advertised as an antiques market turns into a flea market. Crafts dealers and individuals trying to sell antiques and collectibles are best served if they are located in different areas and not co-mingled.

Antiques Malls

The popularity and rise of antiques malls is primarily a product of the 1980s. Almost every community along a major thoroughfare in America now has an antiques mall located in an abandoned grocery or discount store. Many antiques malls have become flea markets confined within four walls and a 10' ceiling.

Antiques malls are designed to provide dealers with the opportunity to rent a booth for a monthly fee. Often the dealers pay a small percentage of their sales in addition to the rental charge. The mall is usually open seven days a week, and the dealers do not have to be present. The manager of the mall or a clerk takes the customer's money and credits the dealer's account when a sale is made. The dealer receives a monthly statement and a check for the merchandise that has been sold from his or her booth. There is often a standard 10 percent discount for customers with a tax number who buy with the alleged intent to resell.

Few of the malls have specialized in particular types of antiques. They tend to be "general line" operations with items ranging from salt shakers to Shaker rocking chairs. If you live in close proximity to an antiques mall you should probably make a weekly walk through. Dealers periodically restock their booths, and inventory changes.

■ Whereas an antiques shop can be located almost anywhere and still have a devoted client list that will make it successful, an antiques mall needs a location with a heavy traffic flow or population base in the immediate area.

■ The quality of antiques malls is generally comparable across the nation with the emphasis on collectibles rather than high-ticket antiques. Route 1 along the Maine coast is lined with antiques malls. The assumption by many visitors is that these malls will be filled with early New England furniture, decorated stoneware, baskets, and textiles. They aren't.

■ Give antiques malls a chance. There are some exceptional antiques malls that have well-lit facilities and quality items for sale. These exceptional malls are managed by individuals with organizational skills and knowledge about antiques.

Hints for Smart Buying

PRICE TAGS

There are many techniques that dealers use to inform the public of the price of a particular item. The amount on the price tag does not necessarily mean that that is what the dealer must have to consumate the sale. Some examples of price tags are as follows:

1.
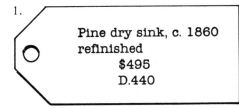

Pine dry sink, c. 1860
refinished
$495
D.440

3.
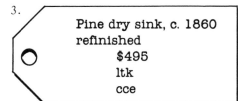

Pine dry sink, c. 1860
refinished
$495
ltk
cce

2.
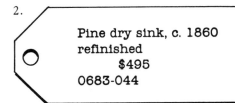

Pine dry sink, c. 1860
refinished
$495
0683-044

4.
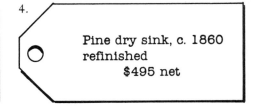

Pine dry sink, c. 1860
refinished
$495 net

Normally dealers are not trying to confuse a potential buyer about the price of the item. The price codes on the tag in addition to the price are for a dealer's quick reference. There are a wide variety of price codes in use, and breaking a dealer's code can be very useful to a potential buyer. The one thing all codes have in common is that they are relatively simple to decipher.

The simplest code appears in Example 1. The *D440* means that the $495 dry sink may be purchased by a "dealer" for $440. Our experience has been that if the dealer wants $440 from another dealer for the piece, you can probably make the same offer and take it home. A "dealer" is someone with a tax or resale number issued by a state. In most states a tax number is easier to get than a bus or subway token.

The second example of the $495 price tag is almost as simple. The number 0683 is the entry in the dealer's inventory list and has nothing to do with the price. The last three digits are the amount the dealer actually wants, in reverse order. The digits *044* translate into a selling price of $440.

Some dealers use a 10-letter word like BLACKSTONE that does not repeat a letter. Each letter is assigned a number, as follows:

B L A C K S T O N E
1 2 3 4 5 6 7 8 9 0

This is the code the third tag uses. Thus, the letters, *ltk* translate into $275. This is the amount the dealer paid for the dry sink. The letters *cce* under the $495 would indicate the $440 "dealer" price. Unless you know the actual 10-letter word being used as the key, this is a much more difficult code to break. For a dealer it has the advantage of the dealer's knowing with a single glance how much he or she has invested

in a piece. The dealer does not have to get out records and look up the inventory number to "see what he or she can do."

"Net" is the final price the dealer must have, so in the fourth example the dealer would not accept an offer of less than $495. No discounts are available in this case, because the dealer has discounted the piece as much as possible already.

Many antiques dealers have a standard 10 percent discount to "members of the trade." Sometimes it is simpler to ask "What is the trade price?" rather than "What is the best you can do?"

RECEIPTS

If you were to go out tonight and purchase a television set for $120, you would carefully bring it home, unpack it, find the warranty, plug it in, and watch a scholarly program about the preservation of the family farm in Uganda. Six months later if the set had a problem you would take out the warranty and quickly find the procedure you needed to follow to get your problem remedied.

If you were to go out tonight and purchase a pine dry sink for $1200, you would carefully bring it home, unload it, and find a place for it. Six months later if you discovered that the drawers had been replaced or the paint was new, you would probably search in vain for a receipt or the telephone number of the dealer from whom you purchased it.

Most of us do not buy television sets emotionally. We buy them intellectually after some comparison shopping. Unfortunately, many antiques are purchased emotionally and without close examination. The receipts or bills of sale that survive the trip home and are saved seldom contain more than the following basic information:

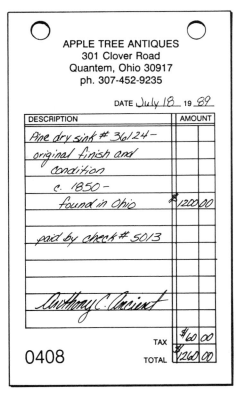

0408 DATE _July 18_ 19 _89_

DESCRIPTION	AMOUNT	
Dry Sink # 36124	$120	00
paid by check # 5013		
APPLE TREE TAX	60	00
ANTIQUES TOTAL	$126	00

A receipt for any antique ideally contains:

1. A description of the piece
2. An approximate date and any available provenance
3. Descriptions of any repairs, replacements, or alterations
4. Detailed explanations of any additions or corrections to the finish of the piece
5. The dealer's address, telephone number, and signature, as well as the date of the transaction

You should have a filing system for receipts. If you buy a piece of furniture, at a minimum you should tape the receipt to the underside somewhere (for example, under a drawer, if the piece has one) so you will always know where to find it if a concern or problem develops later. It is also an excellent practice to pay for your purchase by check. The check documents that you have paid and also allows you to stop payment if you suddenly have second or third thoughts.

Ideally, the receipt should include a more detailed description of the transaction:

APPLE TREE ANTIQUES
301 Clover Road
Quantem, Ohio 30917
ph. 307-452-9235

DATE _July 18_ 19 _89_

DESCRIPTION	AMOUNT	
Pine dry sink # 36124 –		
original finish and		
condition		
c. 1850 –		
found in Ohio	$120	00
paid by check # 5013		
Anthony C. Ancient		
TAX	$60	00
0408 TOTAL	$126	00

DEALERS AND PICKERS

If an individual maintains an antiques shop, it is usually difficult for that person to find enough time to attend farm sales, rural auctions, and flea markets. Many dealers rely on pickers to bring the merchandise to them or to telephone when an unusual piece surfaces.

We are acquainted with a New England dealer who has a shop that is open daily from 9 a.m to 5 p.m. If you want to buy a great cupboard on Christmas Eve at 9:30 p.m., he has six for sale and is more than willing to stay open. The dealer does no shows and advertises infrequently. His merchandise is consistently of the highest quality, because pickers know that he will pay a premium for good pieces brought to his door. He also pays in cash. His business is buying and selling antiques. He does not have time to hunt for them.

Pickers look to this dealer immediately when they find something significant. They know he will not haggle over price *if* the merchandise is up to his standards of rarity and condition. Collectors can be assured that he will be open and probably will have something of special interest to them. They also know that there will be no bargains, but the possibility of discounts for payment in cash is often discussed.

Three Antiques Malls

We have recently visited successful antiques malls in Chenoa, Illinois; Lancaster, Kentucky; and Peoria, Illinois, that provide their customers with ample display areas in well-lit buildings. The Lancaster operation specializes in Americana and the Peoria and Chenoa malls provide a cross section of antiques that ranges from jewelry to country furniture. All three businesses are managed by people who have an understanding and an appreciation of antiques.

LANCASTER ANTIQUE MARKET

The country furniture and accessories in the following section were provided by Rose Holtzclaw and Ellen Tatem, owners of the Lancaster Antique Market, Lancaster, Kentucky. They have provided a sampling of inventory from their 20,000-square-foot showroom, where country antiques are arranged in room settings. The market is located near Shakertown at Pleasant Hill and is open daily from 10 a.m. to 5 p.m. Monday through Saturday and from 1 p.m. to 5 p.m. on Sunday. The Lancaster Antique Market offers a narrated videotape of items that currently sell for $10 (refundable with purchase). The tape may be secured from the Lancaster Antique Market, 102 Hamilton Avenue, Lancaster, Kentucky 40444 (606-792-4536). Antiques are shipped daily by United Parcel Service (UPS) and by freight.

Mustard over red carrier with hand-forged nails; wonderful splay-and-bail handle. **$225–$250**

Early Kentucky mantel in old blue paint, **$300**; pewter chargers, **$200–$300** each; Kentucky long rifle, **$1500–$1700**; early iron lighting.

Kentucky sugar chest with turned legs, unusual "shrimp" color with a dovetailed drawer. **$1800–$2000**

Canadian goose decoy in original paint. **$275–$300**

This early basket is only 3″ deep and 14″ wide. **$150–$175**

Kentucky step-back cupboard, walnut; cupboard has a 2″ step-back, board and batten doors, early red paint. **$1400–$1500**

Shaker sewing box with spool holder and mortised drawer. **$375–$400**

Miniature tin lamp, 6″ high. **$100–$125**

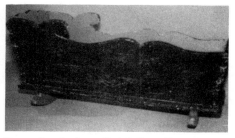

Small basket with notched handles and hickory splint, 7″ in diameter. **$150–$175**

Greene County, Tennessee, cherry pie safe; unusual tins, size, and legs, **$3000**. The cherry drawers on top of the pie safe are from Lincoln County, Kentucky, **$350–$400**.

Pennsylvania dovetailed doll cradle with early red paint and mustard interior. **$150–$175**

Maysville, Kentucky, pottery bottle. **$125**

Maysville, Kentucky, crock with blue decoration. **$350–$375**

Tramp-art box in wonderful blue paint, hinged lid. **$150–$175**

Folk-art box in green and red paint. **$125–$150**

Iron dog doorstop in original paint, some wear. **$85–$100**

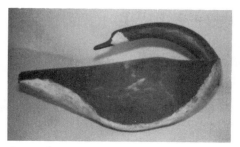

Goose decoy in sleeping position with old paint. **$275–$300**

Long and narrow dough bowl in gray paint. **$150–$175**

Shaker knife and fork box. **$150–$175**

Kentucky bucket bench in green paint; poplar wood with square nail construction. **$450–$500**

Pie safe in green paint with star tins. **$600–$700**

Western Kentucky two-door cupboard in original green paint and cream trim, c. 1840. **$1250–$1350**

Set of six Chippendale reproduction chairs, c. 1930. **$1500–$1700,** set

East Tennessee maple pie safe with drawers and turned legs. **$950–$1050**

Pennsylvania jelly cupboard with dovetailed galley, c. 1850. **$700–$800**

Kentucky basket with hickory splint woven between the wire. **$85–$95**

Very small drop-leaf table with tapered legs in red paint. **$450–$500**

Rectangular basket in blue paint. **$300–$325**

Red, yellow, and blue plaid homespun blanket. **$125–$150**

Seven-inch Kentucky egg basket in old red paint. **$300–$350**

Child's bed made to rest against the side of an adult bed, Shaker-style. **$650–$750**

Amish cupboard in original green paint, ash wood. **$3500**

New England step-back cupboard in old red paint. **$3500**

Jelly cupboard, **$900–$1000**. Blue-and-white appliqué quilt, **$450–$500**.

Stack of Shaker Harvard lap boxes in graduated sizes. **$100–$175** each

Ohio flat wall cupboard in old blue paint. **$700–$800**

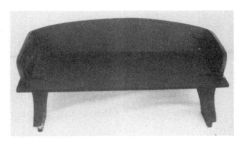

Goat cart seat in green and black paint. **$200–$225**

Green painted bucket with black bark bands.
$200–$225

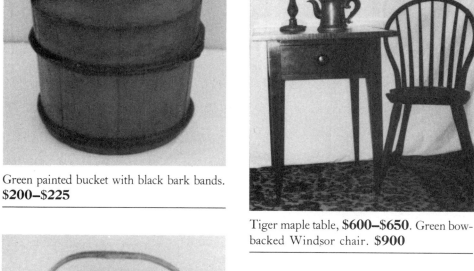

Tiger maple table, **$600–$650**. Green bow-backed Windsor chair. **$900**

Six-inch basket in mustard paint with carved handle and closely woven work. **$300–$325**

Kentucky factory-made basket with heavy wire and double wooden handles. **$75–$100**

Dry sink in green paint with paneled doors and sides; unusual placement of well in top corner with some restorations. **$500–$600**

Early blown lantern with tin base and top.
$200–$250

Step-down Windsor with wonderfully curved side spindles. **$250–$300**

Several storage boxes, all in paint, ranging in price from **$150–$500** each.

Student lamp with original shade. **$250–$300**

Federal-style desk with dovetailed case.
$750–$850

Shaker cheese ladder, Harvard community.
$200–$250

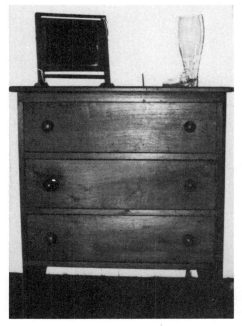

Small walnut chest, possibly made in Kentucky, nice early dovetailed drawers, c. 1800.
$1000–$1200

Walnut Kentucky chest with "moon" inlay on the sides. **$3000–$3500**

Contemporary miniature baskets made in Kentucky. **$175**, set

North Carolina glass door cupboard in red paint. **$1150–$1250**

Butternut step-back cupboard with two three-paned glass doors, painted blue interior. **$2000–$2500**

ANTIQUE MALL OF CHENOA

The Antique Mall of Chenoa, Illinois, is located at Exit 187 from Interstate 55. The mall in Chenoa contains more than 10,000 square feet of quality antiques and is open Monday through Saturday from 10 a.m. to 6 p.m. and on Sunday from 1 p.m. to 5 p.m. (815-945-7594).

Unusual wire candle holder. **$65–$70**

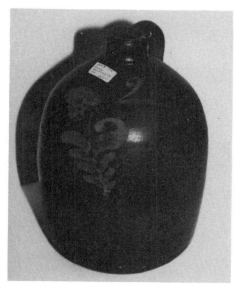

Two-gallon decorated jug, Albany slip and ochre. **$250–$276**

Cardboard Halloween pull toy, wooden wheels. **$165–$175**

Child's chair with original painted finish, c. 1890. **$110–$125**

Five-gallon Western Stoneware crock.
$35–$45

Painted dollhouse, late nineteenth century.
$2500–$3000

Eight-gallon Blue Band stoneware crock.
$58–$65

Child's rocking chair, original painted finish. **$80–$120**

Towle's Log Cabin Syrup tin. **$85–$100**

Porcelain barbershop sign. **$80–$100**

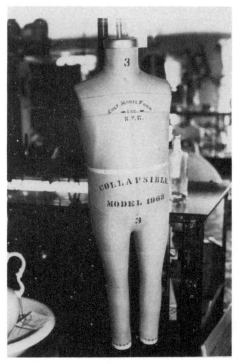

Collapsible Model figure with stand, c. 1900. **$150–$175**

Child's push cycle, painted green, c. 1930. **$60–$75**

Sensation Smoking Tobacco container. **$85–$95**

Egg-O Baking Powder can. **$23–$25**

Old Dutch can. **$16–$20**

Calf brains container. **$15–$20**

Breakfast Call Coffee tin. **$35–$40**

American Home Coffee container. **$42–$50**

Mirex cigar tin. **$20–$25**

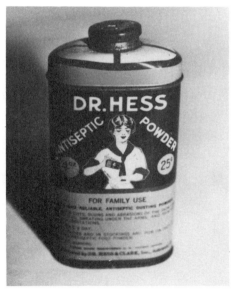

Dr. Hess tin. **$6–$8**

Advo Gold Medal Coffee tin. **$35–$40**

Purity Rolled Oats cardboard container.
$22–$26

White Owl tin. **$8–$10**

Tic-Toc container. **$16–$18**

Crispo Lily Sodas container. **$32–$35**

Metal milk sign. **$55–$60**

Folger's Coffee tin. **$27–$30**

Papier-mâché rabbit candy container. **$35–$50**

Union Leader Tobacco container. **$9–$11**

Papier-mâché whiskey advertisement "snowman." **$38–$45**

Cast-iron elephant doorstop. **$85–$95**

Union Leader Cut Plug tin. **$175–$185**

Little Fairies Baking Powder can. **$20–$25**

Sultana Peanut Butter tin. **$28**

Lion Brand Salted Peanuts box. **$40–$45**

Hershey's Penny Bars box. **$12–$15**

Popcorn box. **$2–$4**

Lard tin. **$30–$35**

Penn's Natural Leaf tin. **$22–$25**

Molded stoneware canning jar. **$32–$35**

Peanuts box. **$7–$8**

Metal Camel cigarettes sign. **$55–$60**

Iron spitoon. **$25–$35**

Whitestone EnameledWare coffee pot, unused. **$50–$55**

George Washington holiday package and container. **$48–$52**

Graniteware double boiler. **$60–$65**

Prince Albert holiday container and package. **$40–$45**

Graniteware pot. **$60–$65**

Metal milk sign. **$55–$60**

Metal scale. **$12–$15**

Graniteware pan. **$20–$25**

The Illinois Antique Center is located at 100 Walnut Street in Peoria, Illinois. The center is five minutes from Interstate 74 and houses an outstanding collection of antiques and collectibles offered for sale by 100 dealers. The center is open 7 days; 309/673-3354.

Refinished pine dry sink, c. 1880. **$425–$500**

Three-drawer "cottage" chest of drawers, c. 1890. **$250–$275**

Oak and ash nursing rocker, c. 1900. **$100–$125**

Refinished pine storage chest with three drawers, late nineteenth century. **$235–$275**

Unusual chimney cupboard with paneled doors, c. 1870. **$450–$600**

Factory-made wall cupboard, oak, c. 1900. **$650–$750**

Refinished pine bucket bench, c. 1880. **$325–$400**

Refinished pine dry sink, unusual size, c. 1900. **$330–$430**

Refinished pine cupboard/dry sink, c. 1870.
$1200–$1400

Refinished step-back cupboard, maple and
pine, c. 1880. **$1200–$1400**

Painted wardrobe, c. 1900. **$600–$700**

Refinished pine hanging cupboard, late
nineteenth century. **$250–$300**

Pine refinished step-back cupboard, c. 1900. **$700–$775**

Child's slat-back rocking chair, refinished, early 1900s. **$55–$70**

Child's step-back cupboard, early twentieth century. **$500–$575**

Molded stoneware crock with lid and "drop" handle, late nineteenth century, with sponge decoration. **$100–$125**

Factory-made fruit basket, early 1900s. **$45–$55**

Budweiser cooler, c. 1950. **$30–$35**

Royal Crown cooler, c. 1950. **$30–$35**

Texaco Fire Chief gas pump, reconditioned, 1940s. **$1200–$1500**

Painted pine mortar and pestle, mid-nineteenth century. **$90–$125**

Penn peanut dispenser, c. 1950. **$50–$70**

Cash register, early 1900s, working condition. **$450–$550**

Fairy Dell coffee container. **$45–$50**

Child's toy train, c. 1920. **$150–$175**

Michigan cash register, c. 1900, working condition. **$550–$650**

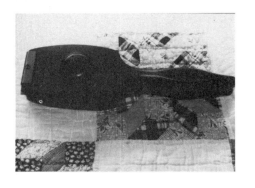

Horse pull toy, c. 1910. **$135–$150**

Child's alphabet table, c. 1940. **$95–$115**

Lemon squeezer, factory-made, early twentieth century. **$50–$55**

Base of feather Christmas tree, c. 1930, stenciled decoration. **$50–$75**

Skor-it pinball game, c. 1940. **$12–$20**

Child's doll cupboard, blind front, c. 1920. **$78–$85**

Factory-made wooden salt box, stenciled label, c. 1930. **$55–$60**

Pay telephone, wall-mounted, original working condition, 1950s. **$175–$200**

Factory-made coffee mill, cast-iron with a machine-dovetailed pine base, original drawer with pull, c. 1890. **$65–$80**

Plastic Santa Claus hanging for front door, 1950s. **$50–$55**

Factory-made washboard. Factory-made metal scrubbing boards, 1900–1930. **$20–$35** each

Factory-made washboard. Factory-made metal scrubbing boards, 1900–1930. **$20–$35** each

Regulator clock, early twentieth century, working condition. **$150–$200**

Mantel clock, working condition, early twentieth century. **$125–$175**

Foot warmer, pine frame, punched tin box, c. 1870. **$135–$150**

Carpenter's box or tray, early 1900s, painted finish. **$95–$125**

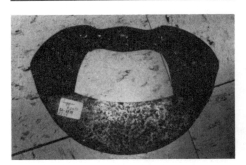

Factory-made chopping knife, c. 1900, maple handle. **$20–$25**

Factory-made butter churn, c. 1900.
$135–$150

Factory-made butter churn, early twentieth century. **$100–$115**

Barrel butter churn, factory made, c. 1900.
$135–$150

COUNTRY
FURNITURE

Brief History

Collectors of country furniture are primarily interested in the chairs, cupboards, tables, pie safes, and dry sinks that decorated the rural and small-town homes of America in the period between 1830 and the late nineteenth century. Prior to the Civil War years, furniture was for the most part made locally and sold or bartered. Much of the furniture was made of pine or poplar, soft woods that show bumps, bruises, dust, and splinters over time. Almost all American softwood furniture that was used in the home was painted. Rarely was a piece left in its natural state. The paint provided a coat of protection for the piece and some color for the home.

There were significant regional style differences in country furniture because the craftsmen who generated the furniture served only local needs and made pieces one at a time, to order. Many pieces of country furniture are adaptations of more formal urban furniture. Bits and pieces of Queen Anne, Hepplewhite, and Chippendale styles were often borrowed by country craftsmen. Rarely was a piece signed by its maker, making attribution almost impossible today. The craftsman viewed his work as a job and his product as a utilitarian and functional item. The completion of each piece was not considered a significant event. ("What was it used for?" is a question that is commonly asked, and many dealers will generate an answer to make a sale. They tell the customer an exotic tale of where a piece came from and how it was used. The reality is that there are many country pieces that are unique and were made for a special use by a carpenter long since deceased.)

The types of furnishings in use began to change after the Civil War because Northern factories that had manufactured guns, tents, and uniforms were left with factory buildings and a large work force and nothing to make. The production of consumer goods in huge quantities at affordable prices, which continues today, began primarily after 1865 (although there were several Eastern factories that produced chairs on a much smaller scale in the 1820s).

The steady growth of factories that produced consumer goods and the gradual rise of mail-order businesses like Montgomery Ward Company and Sears, Roebuck & Company in the 1870s and 1880s began to have a significant impact on the production of locally made furnishings. It quickly became fashionable to order furniture by catalog rather than having it handcrafted in your home town.

This change in consumer buying was amplified by the constant upgrading and development of a nationwide railway system that made delivery to almost anywhere a relatively simple process. By the 1880s a farmer in Nebraska or South Dakota could have an oak dining table and six pressed-back chairs delivered within 30 days from Chicago or Grand Rapids.

For a 50-year period from the 1870s until the 1920s, oak was the wood of choice among most Americans buying furniture. There was an incredible amount produced and much has survived today to be fought over at local auctions and scorned by collectors of American country antiques. At some point in the early twenty-first century this seemingly unlimited supply of oak will become very limited and prices will be astronomical by today's standards. At that point, serious collectors of American oak will be highly critical of other individuals fighting over wood-grained plastic dinette sets from the 1950s.

Original Finish

Today, country furniture in good repair and with its original finish intact is in short supply. There was a mania among "primitive" collectors in the 1940s to 1960s to separate furniture from its finish. Relatively few pieces with their early finishes have survived after being sent to the basement, garage, or barn loft for almost a century.

The growing interest in original finish and condition has sent dealers and collectors in hot pursuit of country furniture, baskets, and wooden kitchen utensils that have not been stripped, refinished, or significantly repaired. As we indicated previously, it is uncommon to find a softwood (pine or poplar) piece of country furniture that *was not* originally painted. It is almost equally rare to locate a cherry or walnut cupboard that *was* originally painted. It is interesting to note that when the primary wood is cherry or walnut in a piece of furniture, the backboards and interior of the drawers (secondary wood) are usually pine.

After 1880, some country furniture

was "grained" with a brush or comb with yellow paint to resemble "golden" oak. Oak was the status wood and pine furniture was easily decorated to look like oak. We found an oak-grained bucket bench in Pennsylvania in the early 1970s. The bench appeared to be considerably earlier in form than its painted finish would suggest. The piece was probably oak-grained in the 1880s over a coat of red paint that had been applied when the bench was made in the 1830s.

It is becoming extremely difficult to find a piece of painted country furniture at a show, market, or auction that is in absolutely original condition with a coat of color that has not been "enhanced," "spread," grained, or completely repainted. If the piece has come out of an attic, barn, or basement, the finish has probably been worn away or damaged to such an extent that some serious restoration dollars will have to be expended.

Furniture that has had its finish enhanced can double in price (although its actual value decreases) if the quality of the work is professional. Enhancing is a scholarly term for touching up the surface with a comparable color to fool a potential buyer into thinking the piece has a complete coat of original paint. Many times a cupboard exposed to a furnace or dripping water in a basement for a lengthy period will lose much of the paint on a side. The enhancing process allows the damaged area to undergo some cosmetic brushing and regain its original look.

A buyer should look carefully at any painted surface for consistency of wear and color. If the rungs of a chair show no abuse or the top of a kitchen table has its paint totally intact, some serious questions should be asked; nineteenth-century country furniture made of softwoods was in daily use and should show obvious signs of wear. As mentioned earlier, cupboards, benches, dry sinks, blanket chests, and tables constructed of pine were painted to keep them from splintering, add some color to the house,

and protect them from any dust and grime. In addition, a painted surface was much simpler to clean than raw wood, which absorbed water and dirt.

Sugar buckets and other wooden household utensils were painted for the same reasons. The handle of a painted bucket should have its finish worn back to the wood from contact with the people who used it. The tops and bottoms of cupboard doors usually show wear from being opened thousands of times. Table tops were scrubbed after each meal, so none survived without having most of the paint washed away and the top discolored from soap and water. Also, if the legs of a table carry no nicks or bruises and have a pristine coat of "old" paint, there is a problem. Table legs get bumped, scratched, and wet, and paint has a tendency to peel away over time.

It is possible to repaint a piece with its own paint by "spreading" it. Spreading is accomplished by using a light coat of remover to soften the existing paint on an area of the piece until it has the consistency of a thick paste. The paste is then used to cover the worn areas.

Twenty-five years ago collectors of "primitives" did not have to concern themselves with problems of original, early, or late finish. When a cupboard or dry sink was found, it was cleaned, stripped, and waxed and then offered for sale or put in the front room. Few people were interested in anything with a painted finish. It is interesting to note that much of the paint that was stripped away 25 years ago is carefully being reapplied today.

When considering paint, it is important to note that color is a critical factor in evaluating any piece of country furniture. Blue is among the most sought-after colors, along with mustard, bittersweet, red, and green. Black, brown, and white are at the bottom of most collectors' paint charts, in terms of desirability.

Dovetailing

Many auctioneers manage to excite their audiences and generate extra money by screaming, "The drawers are dovetailed!" This characteristic always indicates significant age and large dollars to the misinformed in attendance. Often they are encouraged to put down their orange drinks and corn dogs with extra mustard and start bidding.

Dovetailing, which has been in use by American craftspeople for more than 300 years, is the joining of wood at a corner by interlocking triangular cutouts on each board forming the corner. In the early eighteenth century, a single large dovetail was often used to hold a drawer together. By 1800 a series of three or four odd-sized dovetails was commonly used. In almost every case,

when a dovetail is done by hand there is a fine line scratched into the edge of the board to indicate the required depth of the cut. That line is made with a metal pencil or tool called a scribe.

By 1880 a machine was in use that stamped out dovetailed drawers with uniform sides that fit precisely together. The machine did not need a scribe mark to serve as a guide. Hence, the dovetail can provide a ballpark date from which to judge the approximate age of a piece of furniture. The size and number of dovetails on a piece should be closely examined. If the piece has machine-stamped dovetails, you know instantly that it dates from the late nineteenth century at the earliest and was factory made.

"Married" and Reworked Pieces

In the past year we have seen three cupboards that began life as one-piece cupboards and were currently being offered as two-piece cupboards. At some point each of the cupboards had been sawed in half, probably to get the cupboard out of a room or to make it easier to transport during a move.

Many country cupboards, however, were actually made in two pieces. To tell whether the top and bottom pieces of a cupboard belong together, that is, whether they are parts of the same original piece, compare the upper section and the lower section. They should be identical in wood, molding, design, and paint history.

A piece of furniture may be described as "married" if the top of one cupboard is put with the base of another. Step-back cupboards that were made in two pieces are especially susceptible to "marriage proposals." When one half is lost or damaged beyond repair, a semigifted craftsperson can

replicate the missing piece or make over an existing piece, and the marriage is finalized. It is a relatively simple process to marry the bottom of one cupboard with the top of another. It is easier and less expensive to refinish both halves, rather than trying to match the color and wear of the paint or finish on the original piece. What usually cannot be altered to match are the backboards of both parts. The back of a cupboard is almost never painted.

Take an especially close look at the backboards of any case piece (such as a cupboard or desk) before you write the check. If the piece has new nails or holes where there is no purpose for a nail, pay closer attention to the age of the piece. New nails suggest that the piece has probably had major work done to it. The backboards should not be stained or painted and the color and patina of the boards should be much the same. It is *not* uncommon to find original boards of varying width on the back of a case piece. Wood has a tendency to shrink across the grain over time, so the boards should *not* be tightly butted up against each other (if they are, it suggests that the back has been recently repaired or reworked).

Many times a collector is wiser to buy a piece in "as found" condition rather than an example that has undergone major repairs. With the "as found" cupboard that has come to you out of a barn, attic, or home there usually are no surprises. It is what it appears to be. If a piece has had doors replaced, a new bracket base added, or new feet attached, and the job isn't of the highest quality, it can be very expensive to repair.

Notes on Specific Pieces

DRY SINKS

The dry sink evolved from the bucket bench with the addition of doors and a zinc-lined well or trough. Most dry sinks date from the period spanning 1870 to the early 1900s. Dry sinks can be found with lift lids, galleries, and drawers, or with attached cupboards. Most dry sinks were made of pine or poplar; however, some Midwestern sinks were constructed of walnut, and late factory-made examples of oak are also occasionally found.

The wells were originally lined with zinc, but few dry sinks retain the original zinc by the time they make it to an antique shop. If the sink has a copper lining, the copper is a recent addition to the piece.

PIE SAFES

The pie safe or cupboard was used for food storage. The pierced tins allowed air to circulate within the cabinet. Safes were in daily use from the 1840s until well into the twentieth century. After 1875, many were factory-made of oak or combinations of poplar, pine, and maple. It is not unusual to find screen wire rather than pierced tins in late factory-made or handcrafted safes.

We see a great many pie safes for sale during the course of a single year. The vast majority are beat up: the paint is peeling,

tins are rusted through, drawers are missing or broken, and the price is invariably high.

PAINTED CHESTS

Painted chests with three or four drawers in semigood or good shape are hard to find. Most have been banged around, and many were painted each time the wallpaper was changed. Almost every nineteenth-century bedroom had at least one chest, but relatively few have survived. After 1870, factories began cranking out thousands of bedroom sets, and many homemakers relegated country beds and chests to the attic or the town dump and stood in line at the post office to order Grand Rapids oak by return train.

CHAIRS

A variety of woods were commonly used in most country chairs, with each wood serving a specific purpose. The different colors and grains of the woods used made little difference, because the chairs were always painted.

When the stretchers of a chair (or table) are within an inch of the floor, it is usually an excellent bet that the piece has lost some of its leg height at some point. The term "pieced out" means that several inches are added to a chair to give it back its original leg length. The most difficult part of piecing out a chair is matching the paint on the new sections of leg with the old paint on the remainder of the chair.

Many "simple" rocking chairs or side chairs are described as "Shaker." The Shakers were in the rocking chair business for more than a century. After the early 1870s the chairs were mass-produced at Mt. Lebanon, New York. The Shakers continued to make the same chairs until the early 1940s when the factory burned. Shaker rocking chairs were made in eight sizes (0–7). The 7 is the largest and the 0 was designed for a small child. The number is typically impressed into the back of the top slat. The chairs were not handcrafted and are never crude.

OPEN CUPBOARDS

An "open" cupboard has no doors in its upper section and is a very desirable piece of country furniture. It is not unusual to find that an "open" cupboard originally had doors and a blind front. The holes for the hinges are usually filled and painted over or a piece of molding is used as a cover.

COUNTRY BEDS

Country beds are becoming difficult to find. Most nineteenth-century rope beds were made of softwoods and painted. Seldom are walnut or cherry "country" beds found.

IMMIGRANTS' CHESTS

Dating can be tricky with painted immigrants' chests that carry dates and addresses for shipment to the United States. Most of the chests are dated 1850 to 1880 but were certainly made earlier. It is doubtful that many were made specifically for the trip to America. Many of these chests have dome or raised tops to prevent them from being stacked one on top of the other in the cargo hold of the ship. If a trunk had a flat top, it was standard practice to stack other items on top of it, which increased the potential for damaged contents.

An Apocalyptic Tale

Most collectors of country furniture have a serious weakness for drawers, and prices escalate quickly for apothecary chests and spice cabinets with numerous drawers. We admit to having some of this weakness. On a fall day in 1979 we received a call from a legendary dealer in central Indiana who screamed into the telephone that he had just bought the greatest apothecary chest that had ever been found. It was 6' high and 4' wide and had 64 drawers of varying size. He indicated that if we left immediately and made the five-hour drive in four hours, he would hold it for us until we got there.

We should have known better, but emotion overruled intellect, and we made the trip. This was not the first time he had called with the "greatest" cupboard, bed, or table that had ever been uncovered, and each time we had foolishly complied and gone to see what he had found. We had not purchased any of the "greatest" pieces, but he usually had something else that made the trip somewhat worthwhile.

When we arrived at his shop this time, he ushered us in to see the apothecary chest. He had neglected to mention over the telephone that it had come out of an automobile dealer's garage rather than a drugstore. The piece was missing many drawers and a back, and it was heavily covered with oil, sixty years of grime, penciled notations about bolt sizes, telephone numbers, and termite tracks. It was not the greatest piece we had ever seen. It was also priced at $1100.

When we told him that we were not interested, he went into his familiar, regionally famous song and dance about how sorry he was that we had traveled so far and how he was going to make us a deal. The price suddenly dropped from $1100 to $700. By the time we got into the car and turned on the engine, the price had been reduced to $385. He ran after us for a block, and as we turned the corner he screamed that $150 was the best that he could do.

Painted pine storage cupboard, two paneled doors, fourth quarter of the nineteenth century. **$700–$850**

A *cornice* is a decorative horizontal molding on a case piece. In this example, the two side pieces of the cornice are missing. Generally, someone working on the cupboard would remove the front strip rather than attempting to match the missing side strips. The area of the cupboard covered by the cornice usually has "shadows" because its surface is not exposed to light, dirt, or handling and thus maintains more of the original color.

Painted softwood "jelly cupboard," third quarter of the nineteenth century. **$550–$700**

This is an excellent piece of country furniture, but its value would be enhanced if it had a gallery on top and the paint were in better condition. (The decorative skirt at the bottom and the upper drawer increase its value.) A "jelly cupboard" was used in the kitchen to store a wide variety of foods, including preserves and jams.

Painted softwood "jelly cupboard," third quarter of the nineteenth century. **$700–$975**

This is another variation of a kitchen storage cupboard with a single door and no drawers. It is painted a soft blue that adds much to its desirability.

Rare two-door storage cupboard, painted softwood, second quarter of the nineteenth century. **$700–$900**

This is a very desirable piece because of its unusual size and the two doors held by "H hinges," which were hand-wrought and used on cupboard doors only. The cornice also gives this piece an additional positive touch.

Pine closed cupboard, painted finish, third quarter of the nineteenth century. **$475–$600**

Softwood pie safe, painted finish, turned feet, pierced "star" tins, gallery, third quarter of the nineteenth century. **$950–$1150**

This pie safe has turned feet, two drawers, ten hand-punched tins, and two doors. It is also in a condition that allows you to purchase it, bring it home, and put in in the front room. It does not have to be refinished or repaired.

Softwood, two-door cupboard, ogee bracket base, paneled door, third quarter of the nineteenth century. **$800–$950**

Painted pie safe, gallery, tapered feet, fourth quarter of the nineteenth century. **$675–$800**

Softwood "glazed" cupboard, step-back, third quarter of the nineteenth century. **$1000–$1300**

The strips of wood that frame and hold the panes of glass in a case piece of furniture are called muntins or mullions. The muntins should *always* line up with the interior shelves. If they are not aligned, it is an excellent bet that the doors or the shelves have been reworked or replaced entirely.

This is an excellent country cupboard that is structurally sound and has been overpainted. The glass may or may not be original, but it really doesn't make that much difference. Although not so on this piece, the step-back on some cupboards was deep enough to provide a work space.

Pine "high" sink, painted and grained finish, fourth quarter of the nineteenth century. **$1250–$1500**

Other than the shelf, which is probably a late addition, this "high" dry sink appears to be in its original condition. We rarely see legitimately old "high" sinks that have not been reworked with new backs and drawers.

Painted pine dry sink, "bootjack" ends, second quarter of the nineteenth century. **$550–$750**

If you added doors to this sink, it would be a conventional example.

Pine storage cupboard, original painted finish, fourth quarter of the nineteenth century. **$2800–$3200**

This is a rare piece of American country furniture. Seldom will collectors find a storage piece similar to this example, which has three drawers and doors rather than the more traditional two. The additional door on the bottom takes it from a good cupboard to a great cupboard.

Painted pine cupboard, raised panels, second quarter of the nineteenth century. **$600–$750**

It is not uncommon to find the top of a step-back being offered as a hanging cupboard and the base as a "jelly cupboard." This piece is the upper section of an exceptional step-back cupboard that dates from the 1825–1850 period. If it were reunited with its original base, the value of the piece would be well over four figures.

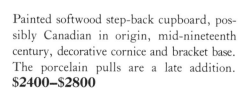

Painted softwood step-back cupboard, possibly Canadian in origin, mid-nineteenth century, decorative cornice and bracket base. The porcelain pulls are a late addition. **$2400–$2800**

Blind-front walnut cupboard, turned feet, step-back form, second quarter of the nineteenth century. **$1600–$2200**

Walnut corner cupboard, blind front, decorative skirt, mid-nineteenth century. **$1400–$1800**

Softwood step-back cupboard, blind front, turned feet, second quarter of the nineteenth century. **$1600–$2200**

Walnut three-drawer chest with glazed bookcase top, two pieces, iron casters on the feet, third quarter of the nineteenth century. **$1000–$1300**

Blind-front cupboard, step-back, one-piece construction, third quarter of the nineteenth century. **$1200–$1500**

Factory-made kitchen cupboard, original unpainted finish, step-back work surface, fourth quarter of the nineteenth century. **$500–$600**

Four-drawer softwood chest, paneled sides, painted finish, fourth quarter of the nineteenth century. **$400–$500**

Painted pine dry sink, zinc-lined well, painted finish, c. 1900. **$500–$650**

This late sink is made from wood held together by tongue-and-groove joints (wainscoting). It dates from the 1890–1910 period and was found in Kentucky. It is a desirable piece because of its unusual size and original green paint.

Painted pine tavern table, "H stretcher," second quarter of the nineteenth century, replaced "scrubbed" top. **$500–$600**

Painted pine chest of drawers, third quarter of the nineteenth century. **$400–$500**

Pine and poplar lamp table, painted bittersweet, found in North Carolina, third quarter of the nineteenth century. **$300–$385**

Pine lamp table, tapered legs, painted finish, third quarter of the nineteenth century. **$225–$275**

Twenty-four drawer apothecary chest, 36″ × 42″ × 14″, original "washed" finish, softwood, third quarter of the nineteenth century. **$1200–$1500**

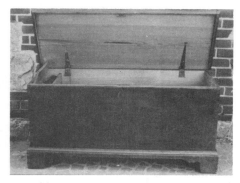

Pine blanket box, painted finish, bracket base, till, second quarter of the nineteenth century. **$600–$700**

Pine washstand, c. 1900, painted finish. **$285–$350**

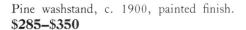

Kitchen table, factory made, fourth quarter of the nineteenth century, painted pine, "scrubbed" top. **$425–$500**

The "three board" top of this piece had its painted finish wiped or scrubbed off over a period of years. Regardless of how long or how hard the top has been scrubbed, there should be traces of paint that match the paint history of the base. The boards on this top also do not have thin horizontal strips nailed to each end. "Bread board ends," or cleats, keep the top from warping. This top does show signs of warping or "cupping."

Maple, pine, and poplar slat-back rocking chair with splint seat, fourth quarter of the nineteenth century. **$225–$250**

It is not uncommon to find a simple rocking chair like this example, with similar arms and finials, described and offered for sale as "Shaker." Be warned: It isn't.

Crude country rocking chair, slat-back, carved finials, painted finish, made from maple, ash, and pine; second quarter of the nineteenth century. **$175–$200**

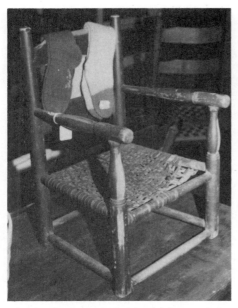

Child's slat-back or ladder-back armchair, "as found" condition, splint seat, third quarter of the nineteenth century. **$150–$185**

Child's rocking chair with taped seat; unusually turned arms, front posts, and back posts; "acorn" finials; mid-nineteenth century. **$165–$200**

Three pieces of Adirondack furniture with cane backs and seats, first quarter of the twentieth century. **$550–$600**

Pine bench, painted finish, "half moon" cutouts on the legs, mortised construction, probably nineteenth century. **$165–$220**

Many pieces of country furniture are extremely difficult to date accurately because the techniques used to construct them did not change much over a century. Handcrafted benches were in daily use and received a great deal of abuse that prematurely aged most of them.

Sycamore chopping block on turned legs, "as found" condition, c. 1900. **$200–$300**

Bentwood cradle, maple, factory made, fourth quarter of the nineteenth century. **$150–$175**

    One of the highlights of the Philadelphia Exposition in 1876 was the introduction of bentwood furniture to America. Many furniture exhibitors were impressed enough to go home and produce their own lines of bentwood home furnishings, and the nation was flooded with chairs, tables, and cradles.

Drop-front walnut desk with bookcase, Midwestern in origin, third quarter of the nineteenth century. **$500–$650**

    It is obvious that the interior of this bookcase has been reworked, because the muntins or mullions that frame the glass do not even come close to lining up with the shelves. The bookcase section originally had only two shelves. It would be a relatively simple task to restore the piece to its original form.

Bedside or lamp table, pine, painted finish, mid-nineteenth century. **$225–$250**

Rustic chair, North Carolina, early twentieth century, painted finish. **$300–$350**

Oak office chair, swivel base, factory made, c. 1900. **$180–$225**

Armchair with a rush seat, late nineteenth century. **$150–$175**

English armchair, variety of woods, late nineteenth century. **$200–$275**

Painted ladder-back rocking chair, c. 1850.
$110–$135

Desk made ("married") from two pieces of turn-of-the-century furniture, cherry and maple, refinished. **$550–$625**

Refinished pine cupboard from Maine, 1860s. **$800–$900**

Storage cabinet for shaving mugs, 12 interior compartments, c. 1900, pine, refinished. **$200–$240**

Poplar and pine pie safe, refinished, Midwestern, late nineteenth century. **$500–$600**

Refinished pine dry sink, late nineteenth century. **$475–$550**

New England storage trunk, possibly used on a ship, painted pine, unusual form, c. 1840. **$350–$500**

Poplar kitchen cupboard, late nineteenth century, refinished. **$350–$450**

Pine cupboard, c. 1870. **$475–$525**

Painted blanket box, pine, mid-nineteenth century. **$450–$475**

Ten-drawer apothecary chest, painted finish with labels, c. 1840. **$1100–$1200**

Unusually narrow cupboard with bracket base, pine, painted finish, North Carolina, mid-nineteenth century. **$850–$1100**

Painted pine cupboard, open front, North Carolina, c. 1840. **$2500–$3000**

Pine corner cupboard, bracket base, mid-nineteenth century. **$2200–$2600**

Unusual open-front cupboard, North Carolina, painted, c. 1840. **$2400–$3000**

Painted pine bucket bench, c. 1860. **$400–$500**

Pine open corner cupboard, 1830s. **$2500–$3000**

Painted pine corner cupboard, c. 1830.
$3000–$3500

Primitive pine cupboard, North Carolina,
c. 1850. **$2000–$2500**

Painted blanket box, "bootjack" ends, pine,
c. 1830. **$600–$675**

Four-drawer chest, mid-nineteenth century. **$500–$700**

3

DECORATED STONEWARE & YELLOWWARE

Stoneware

Collectors of American stoneware evaluate a piece on the basis of decoration, condition, form, and maker's mark.

Most stoneware decorators were paid on the basis of how many pieces they handled during the course of a workday. Few were inclined to spend much time on an individual piece.

After 1870, the competition among potteries reached the point that every possible corner was cut to keep the price of production down, and, as a result, the quality of decoration on most pieces continued to decline. On rare occasions an elaborately decorated piece was created as a special order for a gift or award or was made as an "end of the day" piece by an employee of the pottery.

Much of the value of a piece of stoneware is determined by its decoration. Pieces with birds, people, scenes, or animals are difficult to find today. Generally, the more elaborate or intricate the decoration the more expensive the piece will be. The most commonly found decorated examples carry hastily executed lines, swirls, or simple flowers.

CONDITION

Serious collectors will not consider purchasing a simply decorated piece of stoneware with any chips, cracks, or flaking. On the other hand, if a piece has a battleship incised into its side and is dated "1814," they will usually have a much more liberal attitude about purchasing the piece in a damaged condition. Quality pieces are so difficult to obtain that flaws have become more acceptable and even expected.

FORM

During the first 40 years of the nineteenth century, stoneware was pear-shaped or ovoid in form. An ovoid piece has broad shoulders that taper to a narrow base. Ovoid stoneware was time-consuming to make and difficult to transport, and it gradually gave way to forms that took less time and skill to produce. Collectors are constantly competing for an ever-diminishing supply of ovoid examples.

MAKER'S MARKS

The vast majority of collectors are much more concerned with the decoration, condition, and form of a piece than with where the piece was made. There were hundreds of stoneware potteries in nineteenth-century America; most went out of business due to fires, explosions, or bankruptcies.

The pottery in Bennington, Vermont, went through at least 12 distinct combinations of owners and marks during the nineteenth century. The longest period of continuous ownership was from 1861 to 1881 when it was operated by E. and L. P. Norton. Serious collectors who seek specific marks are especially interested in pre-1840 makers

and stoneware that carries a one- or two-year mark. The E. and L. P. Norton mark was a 20-year mark. It is important to keep in mind that not every piece of stoneware manufactured in the nineteenth century was marked.

BRIEF HISTORY OF DECORATED STONEWARE

Stoneware is largely a product of the nineteenth century, but potteries were in existence in New York City as early as the 1730s (Crolius, Remmey). New York state became a center for many potteries because of the availability of clay and water transportation. The towns of Utica, Lyons, Binghamton, Geddes, Buffalo, Albany, Poughkeepsie, Troy, and Ft. Edward all had successful stoneware potteries in the mid-1800s. From 1880 to 1920 much of the stoneware made was cast or molded rather than hand-thrown. Minnesota, Illinois, and Ohio replaced New York and Pennsylvania as the major states for the production of stoneware. After 1920, few potteries remained due to the common use of household refrigeration, mass-produced bottles and glass jars, and Prohibition.

VARIETIES OF STONEWARE PRODUCTS

Utilitarian stoneware was popular because it could be used for storage, pickling, and preserving food, and it added no taste or odor to its contents. It was also inexpensive, easily cleaned, and readily available in most areas. Most stoneware companies produced a wide range of products. Among the less frequently found items are foot warmers, bedpans, spittoons, poultry fountains, inkwells, flowerpots, pitcher and bowl sets, flasks, milk pans, and mugs. Some notes on the more common items, such as jugs, bottles, and crocks appear below.

Jugs. Jugs were commony made in sizes from ½ gallon to 6 gallons. The 6-gallon jugs usually had double handles. Jugs were used for storing liquids. Examples with pouring spouts rather than round necks contained molasses or syrup.

Bottles. Stoneware bottles were rarely decorated with anything other than a splash of blue cobalt. Bottles were made for breweries, taverns, and stores. Few were sold to individuals. Originally bottles were sealed with cork. The wire lever lid was added after 1892. After 1855 most bottles were molded or cast rather than thrown on a potter's wheel. Few bottles carry a maker's mark, but many have a merchant's name impressed into the side or neck.

Crocks. Crocks were used for preserving, storing, and pickling. Most crocks were from 1 gallon to 10 gallons in size, but 50-gallon crocks were occasionally made. After 1860 many crocks were made with stoneware lids.

Jars. Jars range in size from 1 quart to 6 gallons and were used for perserving and storing foods. In 1892 a wire lever lid was patented. Prior to that date the jars were sealed with wax and had tin or wooden lids.

Jars from the 1890s also had zinc screw caps that were later used on glass preserve jars.

Churns. Churns can be ovoid or cylindrical in form. Most were offered for sale with wooden lids and wooden dashers, although stoneware lids were also available. Churns were commonly made in sizes ranging from 2 to 12 gallons. Many churns are found without a maker's mark.

Batter jugs (pails). A batter jug has a wide mouth and a pouring spout. Tin lids and caps were made for the mouth and spout. Few batter jugs have survived with their original lid or cap. Batter jugs usually were available in sizes from 3 quarts to 6 quarts and were often unmarked and not heavily decorated. A wire bail handle with a maple grip was used to lift the batter jug.

Pitchers. Pitchers, which range up to 2 gallons in capacity, were rarely signed (marked) or heavily decorated. Pitchers were used for storing and serving water, cream, milk, or syrup. Early examples have bulbous bodies, and late examples have cylindrical sides. Albany slip (brown) was used by many potteries after 1875 to decorate stoneware pitchers.

E. and L. P. Norton (1861–1881) floral spray, four-gallon crock. **$450–$525**

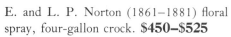

Shortly after the piece was turned on the potter's wheel, the mark was impressed into it. The marks were made from printer's lead type mounted on a piece of wood. If the stamp were dipped into the cobalt glaze before it was applied to the stoneware, it left the mark in blue.

Two-gallon Keene, New Hampshire, crock from the Taft Pottery, 1880s. **$1100–$1200**

This J. and E. Norton jug dates from the 1850–1859 period of ownership. **$800–$1000**

It is important to understand and be able to identify the gradual evolution of forms from ovoid to cylindrical.

The slip-trailed floral spray on the four-gallon J. Norton and Co. jug carries a three-year mark (1859–1861). **$350–$425**

Six-gallon unmarked crock with a pair of spotted birds, c. 1875. **$600–$750**

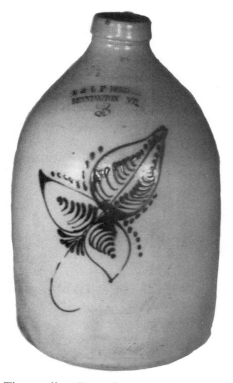

This "shelf" or "porch" jug has the cylindrical sides representative of molded stoneware of the period. **$80–$95**

By 1900 most stoneware jugs were molded, covered with a Bristol glaze, stenciled, and delivered to the distillery that ordered them.

Three-gallon E. and L. P. Norton jug (1861–1881) with slip-trailed orchid. **$500–$600**

Three-gallon widemouthed jar, brushed flower blossoms, N.C. Bell of Kingston, New York, 1830–1834. **$335–$365**

J. and E. Norton (1850–59) crock with elaborate lion, house, and fence scene. **$4500–$5000**

Edmands and Co. slip-trailed deer on a three-gallon crock, Boston, Massachusetts, 1860s. **$2000–$2400**

The zebra-striped deer was also done by decorators at the J. and E. Norton Pottery of Bennington, Vermont. The Bennington deer usually was surrounded by pine trees and a post-and-rail fence.

Brush-decorated 16-gallon Pennsylvania water cooler, unmarked, c. 1860; cooler has the same elaborately brushed cobalt tree on its reverse side. **$3000–$3800**

Unmarked molded stoneware mug, c. 1885, probably from Whites Pottery of Utica, New York. **$100–$125**

Late-nineteenth-century stoneware pitcher with applied molding decoration. **$250–$300**

Yellow desk. **$425**

Illinois folk art quilt. **$2500**

Painted side chair. **$90**

Twelve-tin pie safe. **$1200**

Green bench. **$225**

Decorated box. **$350**

Grained cupboard. **$1400**

Painted dough box. **$500**

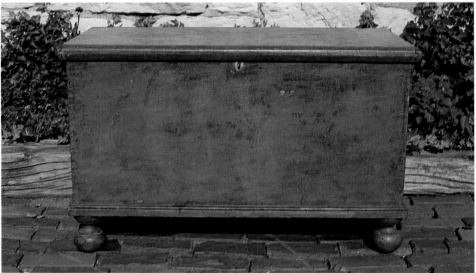

Blue blanket box. **$900**

Child's dry sink. **$950**

Butter print. **$75**

Brush Christmas trees. **$15** each

Coffee bin. **$375**

Copper tea kettle. **$150**

Decorated jug. **$185**

Molded stoneware. **$175–$225**

Stoneware jar. **$425**

Ovoid cooler. **$3000**

Splint baskets. **$100–$200**

Stoneware water cooler with extensive applied molding decoration. **$450–$550**

It was a common practice among European stoneware manufacturers to apply molded decoration to their products. When it was done by hand, it was a time-consuming and expensive process. Many of the American pieces with applied molding decoration were created as trophies or commemorative pieces by special order and are rare and expensive.

In the 1880s, with the introduction of mass production, a process was developed that applied the additional decoration automatically during the molding of the stoneware.

Peacock perched on a stump, slip-trailed, J. and E. Norton (1850–1859), four-gallon churn. **$3000–$3400**

Six-gallon butter churn from J. and E. Norton with a rare date ("1858") in the middle of a floral wreath that is tied with a cobalt ribbon. **$2200–$2500**

Stenciled New Brighton, Pennsylvania, butter churn with cylindrical sides, c. 1890.
$150–$185

Four-gallon butter churn from the Fulton, New York, pottery of Samuel Hart that was in operation between 1840 and 1876.
$1700–$2200

Two-gallon John Burger, Rochester, New York, crock, deep cobalt lily, 1854–1867.
$325–$375

Ovoid two-gallon jar, c. 1823, Bennington Factory (Vermont), brushed "2."
$1200–$1500

Molded stoneware ice-water cooler, Western Stoneware Co., Monmouth, Illinois, first quarter of the twentieth century. **$300–$350**

    This four-gallon cooler was covered with a white or Bristol glaze and then decorated with a sponge dipped in cobalt. The stenciled capacity mark, "ice water," and maker's logo are indicative of many comparable pieces of the period.

Brush-decorated one-gallon pitcher, marked P. Herman, c. 1870. **$600–$675**

Bristol-glazed stoneware kitchen storage jar, early twentieth century. **$50–$55**

Collection of contemporary stoneware decorated with a slip cup from the Beaumont Pottery of York, Maine.

Framed price list of E. and L. P. Norton Pottery (1861–1881) at Bennington, Vermont. **$200–$275**

Most of the potteries developed extensive price lists of their products and distributed them in the limited geographic area they served. Very few have survived today, so collectors must search diligently to locate one.

Molded "As You Like It" horseradish container, c. 1900. **$55–$65**

Molded sugar jar, early 1900s, no lid. **$60–$70**

Stoneware butter container, c. 1930. **$25–$40**

Molded salt jar, 1890–1915, no lid.
$135–$150

Molded storage jar, 1900–1915, no lid.
$200–$225

Molded salt jar, c. 1900, no lid. **$100–$125**

Unusual "thrown" jug, Albany slip glaze, 1880–1900. **$110–$125**

J. and E. Norton 1½-gallon crock, rare "house" scene. **$1500–$2000**

Butter crock, molded, c. 1900. **$100–$115**

Stoneware jug with brushed decoration, mid-nineteenth century. **$225–$275**

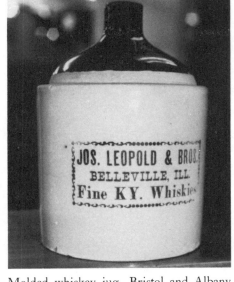

Molded whiskey jug, Bristol and Albany slip glaze, c. 1890. **$100–$125**

Bristol-glazed stoneware jug, stenciled label, c. 1900. **$45–$55**

Molded vendor's jug, stenciled label, c. 1900. **$60–$75**

Two-gallon molded jug, c. 1900. **$30–$35**

Thirty-gallon storage crock, stenciled label and capacity mark, Bristol glaze, early 1900s. **$50–$60**

Burger and Company four-gallon crock, sliptrailed flower. **$335–$395**

Western Stoneware five-gallon crock, stenciled label and Bristol glaze, 1920s. **$60–$75**

Macomb, Illinois, 12-gallon stoneware crock, stenciled label, early 1900s. **$100–$115**

Molded stoneware doorstop, c. 1900. **$175–$200**

A. W. Eddy five-gallon crock, stenciled label, early 1900s. **$100–$135**

Molded water cooler, late nineteenth century. **$300–$385**

Stoneware pickle container, early twentieth century. **$100–$130**

Three-gallon cooler, Bristol glaze with blue striping, late nineteenth century. **$125–$150**

One-gallon butter churn, Albany slip glaze, c. 1900. **$90–$125**

Stenciled canning jar, c. 1870. **$165–$225**

Brush-decorated jar, c. 1860. **$350–$400**

Rare slip-trailed decorated cooler, mid-nineteenth century. **$2500–$3000**

Yellowware

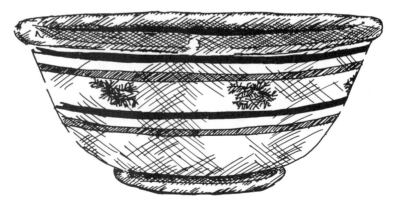

The pictures, prices, and information in this section were provided by Barry and Lisa McAllister, nationally known dealers in yellowware and other ceramics. The McAllisters take part in many of the nation's premier antiques shows in addition to conducting a large mail-order business. They may be reached at Route 1, Box 144, Clear Spring, Maryland 21722 (301-842-3255).

Yellowware is a soft-bodied pottery defined by the color of the clay, which can vary from buff to pumpkin in color when fired. Yellowware was first produced in England and Scotland around 1780 and in the United States around 1830; it is still being produced today. The most desirable yellowware examples are the fairly primitive and mocha-decorated pieces produced between 1840 and 1930 in the United States and England.

Yellowware is usually covered by a clear alkaline or lead glaze, although sometimes the glaze will be yellowish in color. A lot of the yellowware produced was plain in design. Other pieces were decorated with various combinations of colored slip, mocha, and colored glazes. Most yellowware is not marked, which makes identifying the maker and place of origin very confusing.

While prices of all yellowware are on the rise, prices for mocha-decorated varieties have increased the most, nearly doubling in the past year. The demand for yellowware and the scarcity of good pieces has necessitated the buying of repaired pieces. There is nothing wrong with buying a repaired piece of yellowware if (1) the damage is reflected in the price and (2) the person you are buying it from tells you it has been repaired. Make it a point to weigh all factors carefully when buying a piece with a repair or one with more than minor damage, but remember that yellowware is a soft-bodied, utiltarian pottery that was used in the kitchen every day. It was not something that sat on a shelf for decorative purposes. It is unrealistic to think you can fill a cupboard with rare and wonderful items, all in "perfect" condition.

Pepper shakers with blue seaweed mocha. **$450** and up, each

Salts, mustards, and peppers from the period 1840–1920 are extremely desirable and not very easy to find. Salts are the easiest to find of the three, and then peppers, with mustards being the most difficult, especially with the original lid. These pieces are often collected in sets with matching decoration. Expect some rim or foot damage.

Foot warmer, 1870–1900. **$225–$300**

Foot warmers have been found in plain yellow in the form pictured, in a wedge shape, and in a shape that resembles a car muffler. Foot warmers, which are not very popular with most collectors, are not common, but they can be located. Minor damage is to be expected on the edges and at the hole for the hot water.

Master salt bowls, banded and mocha. **$350–$500** each

Mustard container with bands, **$350–$450**. Mustard with rare tricolored earthworm decoration, **$500** and up.

CANISTER SETS (1870–1930)

Canisters were made mostly in Ohio, in one of three styles: white bands printed with black letters; blue bands; and a raised molding made to resemble wheat. The wheat style and the blue-banded canisters are marked with an "H" in a circle or diamond shape and were made by Hull Pottery. The white-banded ones probably were made by Hull also and are somewhat earlier than the other two styles. They are also currently the most popular with collectors, although all canisters are highly desirable. Missing lids devalue canisters, but lids can be found occasionally. It is very hard to assemble a complete set of canisters. Such a set would probably consist of 12 pieces, (a canister and lid in each of six sizes). In the case of the banded sets you could also have a butter crock, a hanging salt crock, and some large open crocks. The white-banded buttermilk pitcher would be an added plus.

Buttermilk pitcher. **$200–$275**
    A complete set of white-banded canisters and crocks would probably sell for $4000–$5000.

"Wheat" canisters: small, **$175**; large, **$200–$275**.

Flour and sugar crocks, **$200–$275**. Bread crock, **$300–$350**.

Small canisters. **$200–$275** each

Hanging salt crock. **$275**. Large canisters, **$200–$275** each

FOOD MOLDS (1850–1930)

Molds were made over a long period of time and with a great variety of designs. The molds showing corn, wheat, grapes, and the swirl are the most common, but even these are getting harder to find. Most collectors have a few molds, and for some people they make up very nearly the entire collection. The molds shown are just a small sampling of what is out there for you to find. Do not pass up an unusual or rare mold just because it has some damage, since you may not get another chance.

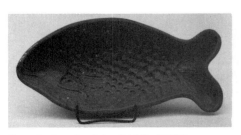

Rare body of a fish. **$400–$550**.

Fruit and flowers, **$200–$275**. Swirl, **$100–$175**. Rare Bacchus, **$500–$650**. Geometric with Rockingham, **$175–$250**. Plain yellow geometric, **$175–$225**.

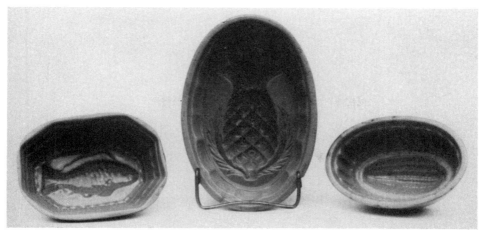

Rare fish, **$400–$450**. Pineapple, **$225–$325**. Small oval corn, **$95–$125**.

Common wheat, **$95–$150**. Rare lion, **$500–$650**. Round grape, **$100–$150**.

Fruit and vegetables, **$225–$295**. Rare fig and stars, **$275–$395**. Rare eagle, **$350–$400**.

Rare bird, fruit and basket. **$500–$595**

Rare roses. **$300–$375**

Unusual corn, **$150–$225**. Rabbit, **$150–$225**.

Rare deer, **$600–$700**.

MINI-MOLDS

These are very small—usually not much over an inch deep and about three inches in diameter. They have been found marked "Yellow Rock, Phila.," a company about which little is known at this time. Most are patterned after tin molds made in England during the same time period. They are very popular but are not commonly found.

Mini-molds. **$145–$225**

NAPPIES WITH SHAPED FEET

These are just like regular nappies except for the feet which are shaped like hearts or flowers. They are uncommon but can be found. Heart- and flower-shaped feet are also seen, less frequently, on baking dishes and pie plates. Look for well-detailed feet.

Serving pieces with heart-shaped or flower-shaped feet. **$175–$275**

CANNING OR PRESERVE JARS
(1850–1900)

Yellowware canning jars were made earlier than most stoneware and glass jars were made. They are not easy to find and have usually lost their lids. Due to their use, most will likely have some rim damage. They can be found in at least 10 different forms and are very desireable.

Canning or preserve jars. **$150–$295** each

PIPKIN OR BEAN POTS
(1850–1920)

Pipkins were made in a variety of forms, usually either with a rounded body with an applied handle or with a wide and shallow body with a long handle, resembling a skillet. They had hard use, so frequently they have damage to the lid and handle. They are very desirable and not commonly found, so consider purchasing one even with damage and/or without a lid if you have the chance.

Rockingham pipkin. **$325–$400**

Plain yellowware pipkin, made in Philadelphia. **$300–$450**

Pie plates, 9″ to 11″. **$95–$175**

Banded bean pot, twentieth century. **$150–$200**

PIE PLATES (1850–1900)

Pie plates can be found from about 7 inches to 13 inches in diameter. They are fairly easy to find in sizes of 9 inches to 11 inches. They are very popular with collectors, especially for lining the shelves of a cupboard. Buy in very good condition unless a marked or footed example is offered. Uncommon sizes and marked or footed examples are $165 or more.

PLATTERS (1840–1880)

There were probably not too many platters made, hence their rarity. Due to this fact, some damage is acceptable when and if you are offered the opportunity to purchase one. They are very desirable and occasionally are found with a Rockingham glaze.

Yellowware platter. **$375–$550**

Oval yellowware platter. **$375–$550**

COLANDERS (1850–1920)

Colanders were easily broken, so there are few to be found. The most commonly seen colander has a molded exterior and a white lining and was produced in England. More rare are the plain yellow or decorated colanders produced in the United States. They are usually shaped like bowls but can be found in some of the forms illustrated here. Colanders are extremely desirable. Expect hairline cracks, especially between the holes.

Plate colander with Rockingham sponging. **$325–$495**

English colander. **$100–$175**

Rare milk-pan colander. **$450–$550**

Rare blue-and-white slip-decorated colander marked "J. E. Jeffords, Phila." **$650–$1000**

Rare basin-shaped plain colander, **$500–$600**. Bowl-shaped plain colander, **$300–$500**.

SOAP DISHES (1860–1900)

Soap dishes are rarely found in plain yellow and are much more common in Rockingham. They usually have holes to drain the water away from the soap, but occasionally they resemble small individual baking dishes. They are often quite plain but sometimes have decorative molding. They had hard use, so most will likely have numerous rim chips. They are extremely desirable in plain yellow.

Plain yellow soap dish. **$295–$375**

FISH-SHAPED FLASK (1850–1890)

A fish-shaped flask is an extremely rare item! A collector would be very fortunate to own one, so damage is not a major consideration. Figural pieces are not found very often in plain yellow.

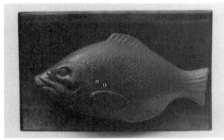

Plain yellowware fish flask. **$1000** up

BOWLS (1830–1950)

Bowls are the most common form of yellowware and also one of the most popular forms for collectors, probably due to their easy accessability and relatively low cost. You can still buy cracked or chipped examples for as little as $10. They are very practical, and many people collect them in multiples.

Bowls were made in sizes from 3½" to 17½". The smallest (under 5") and the largest (12" and over) are the hardest to find and will be at the higher end of the price spectrum. A set of bowls (6 to 10) would also be more valuable than 6 to 10 bowls of different sizes and patterns. Buy the bowls in perfect condition unless you are offered a rare or really unusual example.

Unusual mocha- and slip-decorated large bowl. **$395–$500**

Rare mocha- and slip-decorated bowl. **$475–$600**

Banded and molded bowls vary in price from $35 to $200, depending on size.

Banded and molded bowls. **$35–$200** each

Mocha-decorated bowls. **$250–$650** each

The price is largely determined by the size of the bowl and the amount of mocha on the slip band.

"Tea" bowls: banded, **$95–$150**; mocha, **$275–$395**.

Set of six molded bowls. **$350–$550**

FIGURAL MATCH SAFES
(1870–1910)

Figural match safes were produced primarily in Victorian England. They are usually very ornate, which reflects the style of the period in which they were made. They have varying amounts of gilt decoration which many yellowware collectors scrape off. Some have a white, gritty overglaze. Match safes are not very desirable to most collectors; at this point, however, that hasn't affected the price. They are not commonly found.

Yellowware match safes. **$175–$375** each

4

KITCHEN & HEARTH ANTIQUES

This chapter, prepared by Teri and Joe Dziadul, illustrates items from their personal collection. The Dziaduls have been filling special requests for more than 20 years and offer a lengthy list of kitchen and hearth antiques to collectors and dealers. The current list may be obtained by sending $1.00 to 6 South George Washington Road, Enfield, Connecticut 06082.

Advanced collectors are confronted with the difficulty of acquiring the rare pieces to expand their "interest." Driven by desire, perseverance, and the thrill of ultimate conquest, collectors and dealers continue to set record-breaking prices at auctions. This trend supports the growth confidence shown even in recession periods. With a strong economy, we expect a healthy advancement in items of merit. In many instances, these investments have enhanced the family's financial portfolio.

There is also room in antique collecting for the collector who is not advanced. For the growing numbers of beginning and casually interested buyers, there are modest collecting categories which offer unlimited opportunities to satisfy their wishes.

The Colonial Kitchen

In New England, at the end of the eighteenth century, the kitchen was one of the largest rooms, with a fireplace six feet wide and four feet deep. On one side, the housewife looked out upon the kitchen garden. The kitchen was a comfortable room, cool in summer and perfumed with the scents of the garden and orchard. In winter, it was a cozy retreat, with a roaring blaze of hickory logs in the fireplace as bitter wintry blasts raged without. Fuel was supplied by the surrounding woods, which yielded sweet-scented hickory, snapping chestnut, strong-odored oak, and fizzling ash. If there were no coals from last night's fire and none could be fetched from a nearby neighbor in an ember carrier, the last resort was the tedious task of striking a spark from the flint steel and tinderbox.

Surrounding the hearth were tin, iron, and brass down hearth implements for cooking. Here the cooking was done: meat turned on a spit, bread baked in the beehive oven, and pots hung over the flames in wrought-iron swinging cranes.

Cooking Implements and Storage Containers

The storage of food was of great importance, since food had to be kept from autumn to spring. Cellars and larders had rows of barrels for grains, fruits, and fish. There were shelves of little boxes for rice and mustard seeds and dried fruits. A miniature chest of drawers contained a variety of spices. Lard and suet were stored in tin vessels. Preserves and jellies were contained in stoneware crocks and jars, as were salted foods, fruits, and butter. Salt was a precious commodity and was carefully stored in a box which was hung by the fire to keep the contents dry. Pennsylvania Dutch examples of salt boxes of the eighteenth century are usually carved and sometimes painted as well.

Candles were kept in small chests with sliding wooden lids. Later, tin tubular holders with sturdy straps for hanging and a simple hasp to close the lid came into use.

In the nineteenth century, more elaborate devices and mechanical devices appeared. It was a source of pride to present sweet dishes attractively. Fanciful cutters and molds based on traditional country motifs of flowers, animals, and birds were treasured. Tin cutters were popular for cookies and biscuits. A number of individual cutters were sometimes included in one large circle. A simple round cutter, equipped with prongs, was used just for pricking biscuits. Pastry crimpers may be found in a variety of patterns, ranging from a crimper with a simple wheel at one end attached to a short handle all the way to a crimper made of wrought-iron with a long curved handle in the shape of a bird.

The preparation of fruit inspired some of the earliest "primitive" gadgets, and later, intricate machines. Metacarpal bones of sheep, hollowed out and roughly ornamented, were the earliest implements for coring fruit. Later came cast-iron machines for coring and peeling apples, which were a complicated arrangement of cogwheels and blades; raisin stoners and cherry pitters were also popular devices. Vegetable choppers and herb crushers, other common devices, were cast in one piece with iron handles or wood handles. Some had curved blades which could be used in round bowls or mortars.

Spices were supplied whole and had to be ground at home. Some graters were small and were sometimes incorporated in spice boxes. Tiny decorative tin or wood graters were carried on the person so that nutmeg could be grated into hot drinks and punches. Lemon squeezers were almost always made of wood, since metal was discolored by the juice.

Hanging wall chests: painted red salt box, lid and drawer, c. 1810, **$550–$595**; spice chest, c. 1875, **$350–$375**.

Wood cake stand, original green paint, lathe-turned construction, c. 1875. **$250–$295**

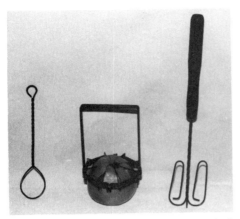

Miscellaneous tools: tin egg lifter, marked "Not for sale," **$10–$12**; green painted apple segmenter, **$25–$28**; Archimedes action eggbeater, **$28–$35**.

Wood chalice, original gray paint with hand-painted black swan, c. 1840, extremely rare. **$1200–$1400**

Crimping tools: wood, carved design on end, **$95–$110**; wood, carved design on end, **$95–$110**; wood, short handle, **$85–$95**; wood, short handle, **$75–$85**.

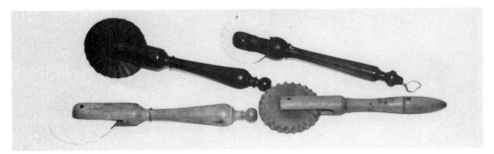

Pastry cutters: all wood, turned handle, **$110–$125**; porcelain wheel, turned wood handle, **$95–$125**; porcelain wheel, wood handle, **$85–95**; all wood, **$75–$95**.

Wood noggins, carved from one block of wood; chamfered or rounded sides, c. 1820. **$135–$395**

They held rum and ale in an earlier period, then cider when orchards flourished.

Lemon reamers: Wood, corrugated head, c. 1875, **$125–$175**; tin and wood, c. 1880, **$145–$175**; wood, corrugated head, c. 1860, **$195–$225**.

Wooden herb crusher, c. 1820; herbs were ground under pressure of roller to a coarse or fine powder for use in cooking. **$575–$675**

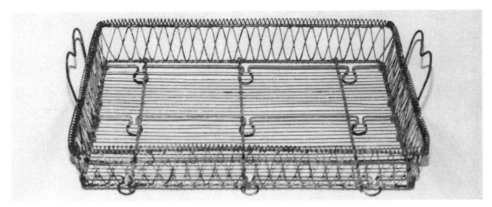

Wire tray, delicate wire design, excellent condition. **$165–$185**

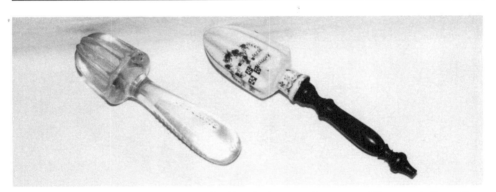

Lemon reamers: glass, marked "Little Handy Lemon Squeezer, Silver and Co., New York," **$95–$110**; china with blue floral decorated head, wood handle, **$145–$165**.

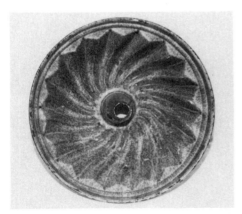

Herb crusher, iron with wood handles, eighteenth century. **$675–$800**

Gray granite cake pan, tubed and scalloped. **$40–$45**

Ice cream molds, brass, used to make oblong shapes for ice cream sandwiches or cakes. **$110–$145**

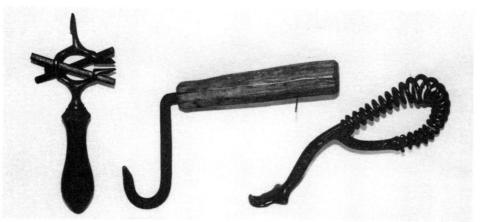

Miscellaneous tools: knife steel, used to put a fine edge on kitchen knives, lid lifter on end, **$28–$30**; pot lifter, iron hook, wood handle, **$55–$85**; stove lid lifter, **$10–$12**.

Miniature irons (children's sadirons). **$22–$30**

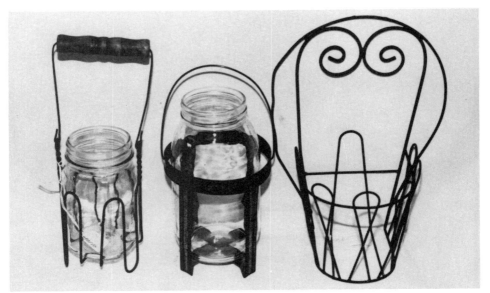

Wire items: wire jar holder with wood grip handle to remove jar from boiling water, **$25–$30**; jar holder, tin with wire, **$28–$30**; wire wall holder, **$45–$55**.

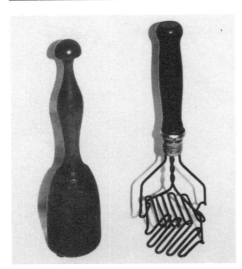

Potato mashers: nicely turned wood masher, **$35–$40**; spring-loaded double-grid masher, **$75–$85**.

Pie lifters, wire and wood, which clamp to edges of pan for removal from oven. **$28–$35**

Spice containers: wood box with inner compartments, **$250–$275**; round container holds 8 dated boxes, Pat. 1858, Newark, New Jersey, bound with tin, spices stenciled in black letters, **$275–$325**.

Spice chest, wood with pewter scroll labels, c. 1880. **$325–$375**

Butter molds: two-part mold, cow design, late nineteenth century, **$375–$425**; hinged variation of above mold, **$350–$395**.

Butter stamps: sheaf of wheat, very skilled carving, **$175–$195**; double thistle, exceptionally well-carved, **$250–$295**; Pennsylvania tulip, c. 1840, **$395–$425**.

Butter stamps and mold: rooster stamp, **$450–$495**; hen without case, **$325–$375**; rooster, c. 1850, with crude repair, **$350–$375**; hen with case mold, **$450–$495**.

Butter stamps: eagle, deep carving, **$495–$550**; eagle, scalloped notched border, c. 1840, **$595–$650**; eagle, elaborate border, **$450–$495**.

Half-round butter stamps: eagle design, rare subject, **$875–$975**; vigilant cow carving, **$875–$975**.

Butter stamps and molds: lily, scarce design, **$375–$395**; flowers in basket, **$550–$575**; stylized pineapple, c. 1840, **$450–$475**; strawberry, blossom, and leaves, **$225–$250**.

Butter stamps, molds, and rollers: individual case, butterpat, cow, **$175–$195**; butter stamp, cow, **$275–$350**; butter stamp, cow with carved name of farm, **$550–$595**; stamp, cow, **$375–$395**; roller, cows, **$295–$350**; roller, cows, **$325–$375**.

Opposite: Half-round butter stamps: sheaf of wheat, **$450–$495**; thistle, **$475–$495**; heart, **$575–$675**.

Butter stamps: rare design, bee skep with flying bees, a symbol of industry, c. 1860, **$550–$595**; rare example of sheaf of wheat, carved fork, rake, scythe, **$650–$695**.

Butter molds: fish, deep carving, c. 1880, **$475–$500**; heart-shaped strawberry, **$350–$375**.

Wood butter dishes and knives: dish without liner, **$50–$55**; dish, c. 1860, without liner, **$95–$125**; dish with blue willow liner, **$65–$75**; dish, unusually large with sapphire blue glass liner, **$145–$175**; butter knives, engraved blades, **$65–$75**; butter knives, steel blades, **$85–$95**.

Shaker boxes: the two-fingered box, **$275–$295**; the three-fingered box, **$375–$395**; the four-fingered box, **$600–$675**; the large four-fingered box, **$1800–$2200**.

Shaker boxes were made using an oval construction with overlapping fingers to prevent buckling as wood aged. Boxes with original paint command the highest prices. The size of the box and the number of fingers also influence price.

Miniature wood pillboxes, 1¼"–4" diameter, for pills or herbs, one dated 1879. **$75–$145**

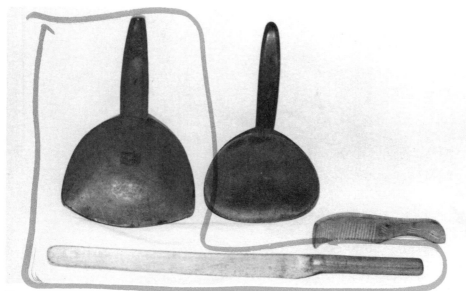

Treenware: butter scoops, **$30–$35**; butter curler, **$45–55**; butter knife to level butter in large container, **$50–$55**.

Treenware: lathe-turned funnel, **$150–$175**; doughnut cutter, **$75–$85**; lemon squeezer, **$65–$75**.

Spice towers (compartmented columns of boxes that screw into each other, c. 1820, scrolled paper labels): six-tiered stack, **$600–$650**; three-tiered tower, **$275–$295**; four-tiered tower, **$350–$375**; miniature tower with grater under lid, **$350–$375**; black enamel with gold lettering, **$395–$425**.

Stoneware jugs: four-gallon jug, lavishly decorated cobalt bird, Fort Edward, New York, **$950–$1000**; sarsaparilla jug, Bangor, Maine, **$125–$175**.

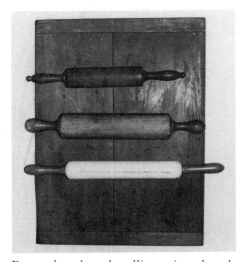

Pastry board and rolling pins: board, **$75–$85**; maple rolling pin, **$25–$28**; maple rolling pin, bulbous handles, **$20–$25**; pastry roller with advertising, **$165–$195**.

Blown-glass jars, with applied glass rings around jars. **$125–$200**

Salt boxes: wood, original red and green paint, **$275–$295**; blue onion with wood lid, mint condition, c. 1900, **$225–$250**.

Blue onion canisters: Prices are judged by condition and rarity of label. Sugar, tea, rice, and coffee are common; these include some unusual ones. In good condition, **$95–$145**; currants, prunes, good condition, **$165–$185**; hominy, damaged lid, **$165–$185**.

Coffee grinder, original green paint finish, c. 1910, Landers, Frary & Clark, New Britain, Connecticut, #20. **$400–$425**

Coffee grinder, red paint, stenciled designs, The Swift Mill, Lane Brothers, Poughkeepsie, New York. **$1200–$1400**

Redware: Jug, dark brown glaze, **$250–$275**; plate with yellow slip decoration, Hannah, **$375–$475**; bowl with splotched markings, **$425–$475**.

Toby salt and pepper shaker, blue willow decoration, left Toby has open salt hat, right Toby pepper pot. **$275–$295**, pair

Toby jug, soft paste, eighteenth century. **$850–$950**

Teapot, double-sided Toby teapot, copper lustre decoration, c. 1890. **$275–$295**

Chop plates, Blue Willow, West Virginia. **$75–$95**

Blue Staffordshire: plate, peace and plenty, mint condition, **$285–$325**; teapot, grapes, European scenery, **$175–$185**.

Pewter items: Morey and Ober whale-oil lamp, **$325–$350**; unmarked miniature teapot, **$175–$195**.

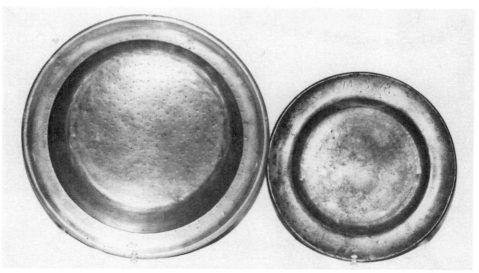

Pewter pieces: deep bowl, **$400–$450**; plate, dated 1722, **$325–$350**.

Coffeepot and teapot: tin coffee pot, **$275–$295**; pewter Morey and Ober teapot, **$325–$350**.

Foot warmer, all wood, perforated designs, tiger maple, c. 1830. **$425–$450**

Pewter charger, unmarked. **$325–$350**

Apple roaster, tin, curved shelves to retain sizzling juices, unusual flat back with handle which raises it up and down. **$535–$575**

Foot warmers: oversized with punched eagle designs, **$575–$675**; punched tin heart decoration, **$300–$325**.

Biscuit and candy tins: Santa and sleigh, **$200–$225**; hearth scene, **$85–$95**; Christmas cottage, **$225–$250**; Santa on rooftop, **$175–$185**.

Samplers: dated 1834, dark-green background, fine condition, **$1200–$1400**; dated 1862, small size, very good condition, **$375–$395**.

Make-do's (broken glass or china objects resourcefully restored to usefulness with a tin addition repair): Toby jug, tin handle repair, **$185–$200**; glass spill holder, tin base repair, **$45–$55**.

Papier mâché: owl with glass eyes, large size, **$125–$145**; double-sided owl with glass eyes, **$95–$125**; ear of corn, **$65–$85**.

Tin chocolate mold, 20″ high, Father Christmas with sack of toys, unmarked, most likely German. **$2400–$2600**

Doris Stauble arrangement, old millinery materials and blown-glass grapes in old wood carrier. **$250–$275**

Doris Stauble arrangement, old millinery materials and wax vegetables in old wood chopping bowl. **$225–$250**

Doris Stauble arrangement, old millinery materials placed in old fruit basket. **$200–$225**

Victorian arrangement, placed under glass dome; compote holds extremely thin and delicate wax fruits, vegetables, nuts, and berries. **$279–$295**

Milliner's model, blue paper bodice, paper cut out eyes, papier mâché body, usually French, used as working models to fashion and display bonnets, c. 1880. **$950–$1000**

Ice cream parlor display, tall copper ice cream soda container, 10″ high, 5¼″ copper straw, 5¢ embossed on side. **$295–$325**

Candle sconce, three-arm copper sconce, signed "A. Cressy, South Sutton, N.H."; Azariah Cressy was a tinsmith who worked in New Hampshire in the mid-1800s. **$475–$495**

Combination copper rack, attributed to Azariah Cressy, South Sutton, New Hampshire; c. 1860, brass plate reads "Spices." **$335–$375**

Copper spice rack and candle sconce, attributed to A. Cressy of South Sutton, New Hampshire; c. 1860, brass plate reads "Spices." **$335–$375**

Skater's lantern, brass with sapphire blue globe (colored globes fetch much higher prices than do those that are clear glass). **$325–$350**

Shaker can, tin, for filling oil lamp. **$95–$125**

Brass candlesticks, King of Diamonds, original pushups. **$375–$395**

Framed candle mold, wood box frame with 12 pewter candle molds, c. 1840. **$1200–$1400**

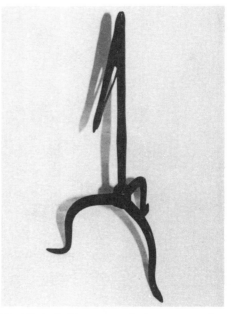

Rushlight holder, wrought iron, serpentine feet, eighteenth century (pitch-pine strips were burned in iron rushlight holders—a two-foot sliver lasted an hour). **$495–$595**

Nutmeg graters: wood, brass, Champion Grater Co., Boston, Massachusetts, Pat. Oct. 9, 1866, **$475–$525**; tin box, storage for nutmegs below, **$250–$295**.

Tin candle molds: 12-tube mold for making short candles, **$275–$295**; 24-tube mold, well-crafted handles, **$450–$475**; 6-tube mold with typical Pennsylvania base and stretcher, **$300–$325**.

Wife, make thine own candle,/Spare penny to handle;/Provide for thy tallow ere frost cometh in,/And make thine own candle ere winter begin.

—Thomas Tusser

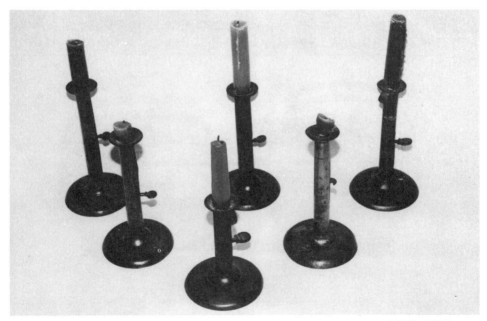

Hog scraper candlesticks, iron with pushups, early nineteenth century. **$125–$175**

Miniature tin candle molds: 6″ high, splayed legs, **$375–$395**; 6¼″ high, tin plate on base reads "Mason's," **$550–$575**; 5½″ high, stretcher base, **$300–$350**.

Miniature baskets: Taconic, New York, basket, **$250–$275**; Maine, Indian splint basket, **$95–$110**; splint basket, **$125–$145**; Curlicue, Maine, Indian basket, **$125–$145**.

Small baskets, ash splint, c. 1880. **$150–$185**

Higgins basket, made in Chesterfield, Massachusetts. **$450–$475**

The Higgins family made baskets in Massachusetts for several generations. Higgins baskets have seen dramatic price increases.

Mechanical nutmeg graters: iron, brass, Pat. Jan. 30, 1877, **$525–$595**; wire, c. 1890, **$175–$195**; cast-iron, marked "Domestic Nutmeg Grater," c. 1870, **$525–$595**.

Mechanical nutmeg graters: tin, handle has storage for nutmegs, c. 1860, **$550–$650**; blue asphaltum grater, c. 1875, **$525–$595**; wood, tin, Common Sense Nutmeg Grater, Pat. July 23, 1867, **$450–$495**; tin, wood, paper label, Brown & Hasler, rotary nutmeg grater, Lynn, Massachusetts, **$695–$795**.

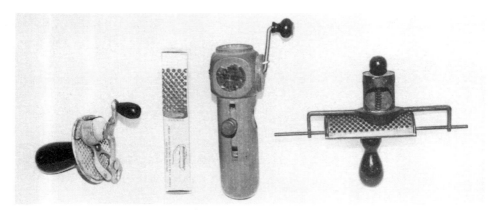

Mechanical nutmeg graters: tin, painted black knobs, c. 1890, **$65–$95**; cardboard box, Stickney & Poor's, tin grater on side, c. 1930, **$65–$85**; Little Rhody, red paper label, wood, **$175–$195**; the Edgar Nutmeg Grater, tin, wood knobs, Pat. Nov. 10, 1896, **$95–$125**.

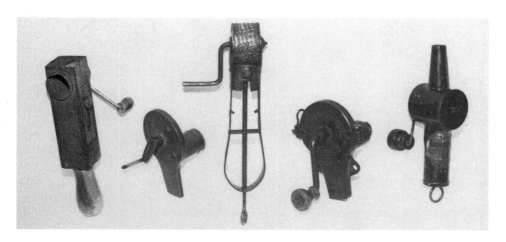

Mechanical nutmeg graters: all tin, Carsley, Lynn, Massachusetts, Pat. Nov. 20, 1855, **$550–$650**; tin, F. Edw. Snyder, Massilon Ohio, **$525–$595**; tin, wood, spring-loaded, later nineteenth century, **$375–$400**; tin, late nineteenth century, **$495–$575**.

Graduated set of early tin graters, hand-punched tin, 1840–1860. **$65–$95**

Mechanical nutmeg graters: tin and wood, barrel-shaped housing on end to slide nutmeg across grating surface, c. 1859, **$165–$185**; tin and wood, impressed "M. H. Sexton, Utica, NY, Pat'd. May 1896," **$895–$995**; all tin, Pat. Nov. 1855, **$375–$395**; wood and tin grater, **$325–$375**.

Opposite: Mechanical nutmeg graters: tin, wood handle, c. 1870, **$295–$325**; tin, bellows-shaped grater, **$450–$550**; tin, spring-action grater, **$395–$425**; cast-iron, brass closure, Pat. June 1870, **$295–$350**; tin, brown asphaltum, The Rapid Nutmeg Grater, c. 1880, **$350–$395**.

5

COLLECTING
COUNTRY
ANTIQUES

Candle molds were the first antiques that we collected seriously. We were able to find a wide variety of configurations ranging from single tube molds to candle molds with as many as 64 tubes. It is amazing now in reflecting back on that period how excited we became when we found a mold that we had not previously encountered.

Our mission in life at that point was to uncover a 12-tube candle mold with the tubes arranged in a circular pattern. We found one for $235 in 1968 in an antiques shop in northern Illinois. The $235 was a dilly of a price to pay at that point, but we had vowed to buy the first "good" one we found, regardless of the cost.

Since 1968 we have been across the nation several times buying country antiques. Over that period we have made a great many purchases but none that was as satisfying or as emotionally gratifying as the circular candle mold.

CANDLE MOLDS

Many tin candle molds have 12 tubes arranged in a 2 × 6 pattern and are usually not difficult to find. The rarer molds have an odd number of tubes (3, 5, 7, or 9) or a great many (36, 48, 64, even 124). In recent years we have not seen any exceptionally large molds or really unusual examples.

The most costly molds have redware or pewter tubes in a wooden frame. These date from the first half of the nineteenth century and were used primarily in New York state and Pennsylvania.

As is the case with almost all antiques, condition is critical in evaluating a candle mold. If the 12-tube tin mold you find in a shop is broken or badly rusted, it should not be purchased. The same decision should be made if the tin mold is painted black. In the 1970s there were several firms that made new 12-tube tin molds and sold them in candle-making kits. We have seen several of these molds painted flat black and offered as "old."

Twelve-tube candle molds, 1860s. **$75–$95**

BUTTER CHURNS

Butter churns were in daily use in many homes from the eighteenth century through the first quarter of the twentieth century. Churns can be found made of stoneware, wood, tin, and glass.

Wooden churns are staved or constructed of individual strips of pine held together by bands of wood, metal, or wire. Factory-made churns began to appear in huge quantities after the Civil War (1865) when factories turned to producing consumer goods.

Stoneware churns were in use throughout the nineteenth century and were highly susceptible to damage. Unlike wooden churns, stoneware examples could not be repaired and were usually thrown away. Stoneware churns from prior to 1850 tend to be pear-shaped or ovoid in form; stoneware churns were cylindrical by 1880. Heavily decorated stoneware churns are rare and valuable from the 1820 to 1875 period.

The glass churns were factory made and largely designed to be used on counter- or tabletops. They also usually used a series of revolving paddles rather than a dasher to produce the butter.

There have been many wooden churns imported from Spain and Mexico that appear to be much older than they are. Most are more cylindrical and crudely crafted than American butter churns.

Factory-made butter churn, staved construction, original lid with piggin handle and dasher, c. 1880. **$200–$250**

UTENSIL BOXES

Twenty years ago collectors of "primitives" usually wrote their first checks for a pie safe, a dry sink, a coffee grinder, a butter paddle, a butter mold, and a knife and fork box. Many of these utensil boxes were pine and painted, with dovetailed corners and splayed sides. The most expensive were made of walnut or cherry.

Painted pine utensil box, nailed corners, fourth quarter of the nineteenth century. **$70–$75**

SHAKER BOXES

Fingered boxes were made and sold in many of the New England Shaker communities throughout the nineteenth century. The boxes were made of pine and maple and formed around molds. At least 12 unmarked sizes were offered in the sisters' shops, along with a myriad of other sewing and kitchen-related items. The Shaker sisters' shops were designed for tourists and visitors to the communities.

The fingers on Shaker boxes were not a decorative addition to the boxes. They were designed to allow for the expansion and contraction of the wood so it would not crack. The fingers were held to the sides of the box with copper tacks. Copper was used because it would not rust and disintegrate and would not discolor the box. The boxes were used for storage of pins, needles, dry cereals, and household odds and ends.

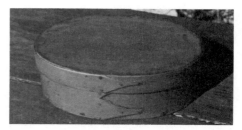

Shaker oval box, painted maple sides and pine top and bottom, nineteenth century. **$850–$1000**

Dry measure, probably New England Shaker in origin, painted maple sides with pine bottom, "Harvard-type" single finger. **$500–$600**

SUGAR BUCKETS

The standard so-called sugar bucket was used for storing a wide variety of items in late nineteenth-century America. Plums, mincemeat, sugar, flour, ground spices, and cereals were commonly put into the factory-made covered buckets. Sugar buckets are staved and held together with wire, wooden, or metal bands (hoops). They have wooden or wire drop or bail handles and were made in at least a dozen or more sizes by more than a hundred woodenware factories. Few are "signed" or marked with the name of the company that manufactured them. Those that are marked carry the impressed mark on the top of the lid or on the bottom of the bucket.

Painted buckets are much more desirable than natural or unfinished examples. Blue, red, yellow, bittersweet, and green are considered highly collectible, while brown, black, and white are of lesser interest to most collectors.

Painted sugar bucket with wooden drop handle, fingers, staved construction, pine, 1880s. **$250–$285**

If a late-nineteenth-century homemaker took the trouble to label the contents of her bucket (in this case, "Ginger") she enhanced its value to today's collector. **$285–$300**

F. H. Jarden of Philadelphia packaged and sold his "Golden Drop Plums" in this bucket during the 1870–1900 period; the intact label adds considerably to the value of this container. **$250–$275**

The Shakers occasionally used a technique described by Mary Earle Gould as "buttonhole hoops" to keep butter boxes and sugar buckets tight. **$350–$425**

The Shakers offered a variety of sizes of staved wooden buckets and pails in the sisters' or gift shops at several of their New England communities. Shaker buckets and pails are distinguished by the metal diamond-shaped supports or braces on the sides. **$300–$350**

BUTTER MOLDS AND STAMPS

Butter molds were designed to provide form and a decorative topping to butter made for use at the table. Butter prints or stamps left only a decoration and did not shape the butter.

The value of a butter mold or print is largely determined by the design it has had carved or mechanically impressed into its surface. Animals, people, and scenes are rare. Leaves and geometric designs are common.

Molds and stamps primarily date from about 1840 to the early 1900s. In recent years many imported molds and prints have confused the market for many collectors.

Rare, carved deer butter stamp, c. 1860. **$575–$600**

Handcarved pointed star butter stamp, 4½″ diameter, c. 1860. **$350–$375**

Deeply carved tulip and leaves butter stamp, c. 1850, **$550–$595**. Hand-carved "hearts" butter stamp, 3½″ diameter, c. 1850, **$350–$395**. "Rose" design butter stamp, hand carved, maple, **$350–$375**. Unusual heart-shaped butter stamp, c. 1860, **$165–$185**.

Machine-carved flower and leaves butter stamp, 1870s, **$375–$395**. Machine-carved swan, 5″ diameter, 1870s, **$475–$550**. Hand-carved heart and leaves, c. 1860, **$375–$450**.

Hand-carved maple butter mold, rare bird decoration, c. 1860, **$445–$495**. Hand-carved "sheep" buttermold, c. 1860, **$675–$700**.

Machine-made flower and leaves butter stamp, c. 1880. **$350–$375**

Machine-impressed American eagle butter stamp, c. 1890. **$500–$625**

WOODENWARE

In 1942 Mary Earle Gould's *Early American Woodenware* was initially published. There were very few collectors of woodenware at that point, and Gould was able to drive around New England and purchase almost anything she wanted. The book is heavily illustrated with items that are impossible to locate today.

We wrote to Gould in the mid-1960s and tried to purchase some of the pieces in the book. She wrote back that the only items for sale were hand-carved clothespins for $4 each. Gould left her collection to the Hancock (Massachusetts) Shaker Museum, and much of the collection has since been sold at auction.

Handcrafted pre-1850 American woodenware is a challenge to find. Like many items in daily use, wooden bowls, spoons, and plates were repaired until they had to be used as kindling or thrown away. After Sears, Montgomery Ward, and other mail-order houses began offering mass-produced kitchen utensils, handcrafted items disappeared (were replaced) even more rapidly.

In recent years there has been such a wealth of imported kitchen antiques that many collectors have been repeatedly fooled.

Handcrafted wooden herb crusher from the Gould collection, used to grind dried herbs into powder for use in cooking, c. 1820. **$750–$825**

Late-nineteenth-century factory-made breadboards. **$195–$250** each

Wooden Shaker apple peeler, signed "SJS," nineteenth century. **$975–$1150**

Walnut cookie board, possibly European in origin, late nineteenth century. **$225–$250**

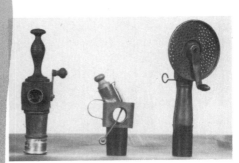

Factory-made maple mixing bowls, lathe-turned, painted finish, late-nineteenth–early-twentieth century. **$175–$225** each

UTENSILS

Collection of nutmeg graters, c. 1860. **$400–$600** each

Variety of hand-forged food choppers, early nineteenth century. **$100–$125** each

ODDS AND ENDS

It is interesting but probably pointless to speculate how a particular item survived intact over almost a century in a society that cleans out the basement and attic every spring and has a garage sale on every block each Saturday morning.

When we brought this rocking horse into our house, our youngest son was about five and absolutely refused to enter any room in which the "pony" was allowed to graze!

The horse was initially carved out of pine and glued together in sections. A horsehide cover, real tail, mane, and ears were added to a leather saddle and bridal and steel bit. The rockers bolt on to a wheeled platform that can be pushed across the floor. It is over six feet long from rocker to rocker.

Rocking horse, original condition, c. 1890. **$3000–$4500**

Iron horseshoe weight with cigarette advertisement, used to keep newspapers from blowing away. **$200–$250**

In our town there is no sidewalk newspaper stand or cigar store that carries newspapers and magazines. Our options are limited to the offerings of a franchised bookstore in a huge shopping mall or machines that are consistently broken, out of newspapers (or both) at several nearby convenience stores.

The cast-iron "Clown Cigarettes" horseshoe with a handle was a weight designed to hold down the newspapers at an outside newsstand in St. Louis, Missouri. It was patented and dates from about 1900. It is one of the items we see occasionally and love, but it falls into the category of "what are you going to do with it?"

Reproduction cast andirons of Revolutionary War soldiers, early 1900s. **$65–$75**

Every dime store in America sold these pressed-cardboard jack-o-lanterns in 1950 for 29¢. You could put a candle in one and probably burn the house down or carry one for candy on October 31—if you didn't have much of an appetite. With the growing interest in holiday "antiques," these paper

Pressed cardboard Halloween pumpkin heads, 1940s–mid-1950s. **$45–$55** each

pumpkins now have semisignificant value and are in great demand.

This hanging cabinet began life as a factory-made spice box. At some point, due to damage or experimentation, it lost six drawers and gained a mirrored door and two shelves. The machine-stamped decorative piece at the top of the cabinet came from a chest and needs to be fitted a little closer as it hangs over on one side.

Wall cabinet made from a mass-produced spice box, 1880–1900. **$125–$140**

SEED BOXES

There are an abundance of labeled product boxes from the fourth quarter of the nineteenth century and the first decade of the twentieth century (1875–1910) that are highly prized and eagerly sought by collectors. Seed boxes were furnished by the manufacturers to the grocery or hardware store and placed on the counter filled with packets of seeds. For a box to be of interest it should have a colorful paper exterior and interior label. This Hiram Sibley box was purchased in Pennsylvania filled with its original seed bundles and packets. We were foolish enough to write a column extolling the virtues of seed boxes for *Country Living,* and prices escalated and the boxes disappeared.

The early seed boxes (1830–1850) were hand-dovetailed.

Factory-dovetailed Shaker seed box, 1890–1895.

Hiram Sibley seed box, interior and exterior paper labels, c. 1900. **$325–$350**

SPOOL CHESTS

If we had to choose between the refinished J.P. Coats spool chest and the overpainted spool chest, we would lean toward the chest that needs the work, even if the price tags were identical. The repaired and refinished chest would have little interest for us because its history was stripped away. It is in better shape today than it was 80 years ago when it came out of the factory. With the overpainted chest you can be reasonably sure that the chest is original and probably has a legitimate patina under the paint.

Refinished J. P. Coats spool chest, oak, c. 1900. **$400–$500**

Overpainted spool chest, oak, c. 1900.
$300–$340

COUNTRY STORE ANTIQUES

It takes some knowledge to buy country store antiques with confidence. A particular tobacco tin may be very common in design, but if it is of a color in which few were made, it is a rare (and thus more valuable) tin.

A serious collector would describe this tin as "flawed," because it has scratches and minor rust. The damage may make it worth only a fraction of what a mint example might bring.

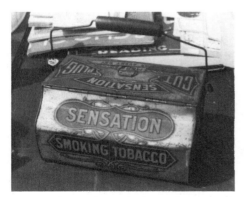

Sensation Smoking Tobacco, c. 1915.
$30–$35

AUTOMOBILE ANTIQUES

There is a growing market for collecting automobile and service station–related antiques. To date we have not been bitten by the bug and have difficulty understanding it. It is inevitable that you will see something like this on the cover of *Country Living*.

Metal motor oil display rack and empty oil cans, c. 1950. **$150–$175** complete

Plywood birdhouse, indeterminate age (another potential cover for *Country Living*).
$35–$45

It's not American folk art, but it's a rare and collectible mode of sidewalk transportation. **$400–$475**

In 1953, Wesley "Chip" Hanback, who lived on Leland Street in Bloomington, Illinois, owned a black Hopalong Cassidy bicycle complete with matching guns and holsters on the handlebars. Chip had the best bicycle ever seen on the east side of Bloomington, but this has to be the premier tricycle.

Screen doors with stenciled advertisements and metal Pepsi "kick" from the 1930s–1940s. **$175–$200** each

GRANITEWARE

The information below is taken from the catalog of Manning, Bowman, and Company of West Meriden, Connecticut, about 1890:

The declining popularity of metal tea and coffee pots has been noticeable for many years. Manning, Bowman, and Company have tested various materials for making an article to meet the growing objections urged against the common ware. In the Perfection Granite Ironware they offer vessels absolutely faultless for preparing and serving in a state of purity the highly prized beverages of the table.

The Granite coating is an insoluble glaze, vitrified under an intense heat, and receives its mottled finish from a liberal mixture of iron oxide. The material being a non-conductor of heat and cold, this ware is especially and equally valuable for keeping beverages at either extreme of temperature.

Graniteware, which was mass-produced in huge quantities between 1860 and 1930, replaced cast-iron kettles and cooking utensils and tinware in most American homes. It is often called enamelware, agateware, porcelain ware, glazed ware, or speckle ware. Granite Ware and Agate Ware were trade names that became standard names for all similar wares.

Rare granite items include meat grinders, canister sets, preserve jars, stoves, ice boxes, and sinks. Miniature sets for children were also made. Pieces trimmed with pewter or another white metal, which date from 1870 to 1900, are especially collectible. Items with cast-iron handles date from the 1870 to 1890 period, whereas items with wooden handles date from 1900 to 1910.

Flour sifter. **$50–$55**

Large cobalt pail. **$150–$165**

Blue-and-white swirl bucket. **$75–$85**

Cream or milk pail. **$185–$215**

Cobalt teapot. **$200–$225**

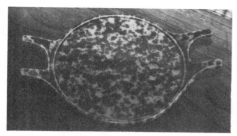

Griddle. **$135–$150**

Serving or making dish. **$75–$95**

Teapot, **$75–$100**. Coffeepot, **$75–$100**.

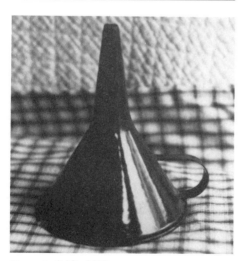

Funnel. **$40–$50**

Soap dish. **$50–$60**

Six-inch gray granite pail. **$55–$65**

Two-gallon bucket with a light blue swirl. **$85–$100**

Cobalt coffeepot. **$135–$150**

Cobalt dipper, **$75–$85**.
Strainer, **$35–$45**.

COUNTRY BASKETS

Splint basket painted red and white, nailed rim, early twentieth century. **$150–$200**

Eight-inch blue grater. **$60–$70**

Miniature melon basket, white oak splint.
$100–$125

Painted oak splint basket with wrapped rim, notched handle. **$150–$175**

Factory-made half-bushel basket, wire handles, c. 1930. **$55–$60**

Eight-inch buttocks basket, unusual double handle, rib construction. **$240–$285**

Gathering basket with machine-cut splint and nailed rim, carved handle. **$70–$85**

Ash splint gathering basket. **$100–$135**

Nineteenth-century buttocks basket, carved handle, rib construction. **$225–$300**

Melon basket with a thickly carved handle, rib construction with white oak splint. **$150–$175**

Melon basket, oak splint. **$175–$200**

Cross section of unusual Indian and splint baskets, southeastern United States. **$145–$350** each

Native American baskets from North Carolina, early twentieth century. **$300–$350** each

Early twentieth-century Native American basket. **$300–$350**

Oak splint bed mat, southeastern United States, late nineteenth century. **$300–$375**

RECENT AUCTION PRICES OF ADVERTISING ANTIQUES

The items that follow were sold at auction in September 1988 by Frank's Antiques. Information about periodic auctions of advertising and paper antiques conducted by Frank's Antiques may be secured by writing Box 516, Hillard, Florida 32046.

Unusual egg-gathering basket with "cheese" weave construction. **$400–$500**

Grocery or food basket with double "dropped" handles, oak splint, unusual form. **$200–$250**

Coca-Cola sign. **$104**

Well-made field basket from North Carolina, oak splint with heavily wrapped rim. **$200–$240**

P.O.C. Beer paper sign. **$10**

Program from Buffalo Bill's Wild West Show. **$175**

Planters Mr. Peanut advertising: mug, **$37**; salt and pepper, **$134**; ash tray, **$78**.

Three paper toys: black child, **$90**; monkey, **$62**; cowboy, **$51**.

Tobacco packages: Navy, **$5**; Parrot, **$25**; Pep, **$11**; Pinch Hit, **$48**; Plow Boy, **$12**; Ramrod, **$5**; Red Man, **$16**; Scrapple, **$5**.

Coca-Cola sign. **$150**

Uneeda Biscuit and Graham Crackers signs. **$85** each

Goldenson Furniture sign, **$18.50**. "No Hunting" sign, **$17.50**.

Tiger seed sign, **$100**. Whistle Soft Drink sign, **$100**.

Metal Pinch Hit sign. **$300**

Revel Ice Cream sign, **$10**. Dr. Pepper, **$8.50**.

Three orange crate labels, **$6–$8** each. Pop Kola sign, **$22**.

6

COLLECTING DUCK DECOYS

What to Collect?

We can add but little to the beginner's rule of decoy collecting: Buy only what you like and can afford! No beginner is expert enough to select the "best" or "most collectible," nor are we convinced that such a thing even exists. We believe that the beginner should buy only what appeals— to the heart more than the head. If that folksy beat-up piece of wood will look good on your pie safe, buy it. No one else will look at it more than you will, so it's your feelings that are important. If your taste runs to a new, perfectly carved and painted piece, then buy that. It will look great on the mantle. If you like it you should have it, if you can afford it. If not, buy something less expensive and gradually work up.

This section was prepared by John and Mary Purvis, well-known dealers of antique duck decoys. They participate in many shows across the nation, selling to dealers, collectors, and "novices." They maintain a mail-order business out of their home at 50609 Bellfort Court, New Baltimore, Michigan 48047. Their telephone number is 313-725-2179.

Paint

Fine original paint (or something slightly less) almost always increases the value of a decoy. Repaint almost always decreases the value. Keep in mind that these are *resale* values. More important to the novice collector should be the value to himself or herself. Antique decoys are "working" decoys, used by hunters. Toss a decoy in and out of a boat 20 times a year for a generation and the paint will be less than perfect. If the decoy has been repainted, the job was probably done by the hunter, sometimes very well, but more often to the hunter's own taste with whatever paint was available. Some decoys from certain areas are almost never found in original paint. For these the quality of the repaint can be quite important.

We do not believe that paint quality needs to be very important to the novice collector. The purist collector, someone with a large collection and a wallet to match, will probably insist on original paint. This can be expensive, especially at auctions. The average collector, including the novice, should be more impressed by the personal appeal of the decoy overall than by the paint. Many collectors prefer the "character" that the less-than-perfect paint gives the decoy. It is important to remember that if resale value is critical, knowledgeable advice is always helpful.

Folksy old East Coast goose, has no paint left; value is in style and character, unusual keel arrangement. **$100–$175**

Pair of mallards attributed to Shannon Crier of southwestern Ontario. Original paint, good carving, and mellow patina. The price on a pair like this is determined more by love, desire, and greed than by past statistics.

Canvasback drake, Marine City, Michigan, 1930s. The paint in this hunting area was put on with a stipple effect not seen elsewhere. Visible wear can limit value. Unusual keel; very heavy for use in swift waters. This example in present condition, **$100–$200**. If perfect paint, $200 and up.

Structural Condition

The novice collector should remember that the decoy he or she is buying was used, probably none too gently. Bruises, dents, scratches, rubs, shot holes, cracked necks, lost eyes, broken tails, and similar hurts happen to a well-used decoy. These "flaws" can and do add character to the decoy and add the appeal of something actually made to be used. The "flaws" can and do lower resale value. They also lower cost. Few people who "find" the perfect decoy, carved and painted decades earlier, will be able to afford that decoy.

The most frequently asked question about decoy condition regards the keel. Should it be on or off? We believe that for the novice this should be a purely personal preference. Many decoys look and show off best with the keel off. After all, it was under water and not seen when the decoy was in use. We would *not* remove the keel from an expensive decoy, just to be "resale safe." For low-priced or moderately priced decoys we feel that removal of the keel should depend on the buyer's opinion of how the de-

coy looks. At least half of the decoys we get already have the keels removed (many decoys never had keels to begin with). In the price ranges we are focusing upon, the value of the decoy will rarely be affected by the absence of a keel. Keep in mind that it is your decoy. You should have it anyway you want it.

By now the obvious should be readily apparent. We believe that if someone is not an experienced collector, knowing item and worth, that person should buy decoys that appeal and give personal pleasure. If a decoy has character flaws, then at the very least we know that it does have character. If a novice one day desires to "upgrade" a collection, then time should be taken for study in order to establish preferences, reevaluate price scales and concerns, locate knowledgeable advisors, and learn the market. That person's collection will then change, and there may even be a few "perfect" decoys on the shelf. Remember, though, that the most perfect decoy may not tell the best tales.

Canvasback drake made by Fern Buck. Oversized and in the original paint with a classic head. **$200**

Pair of goldeneye from Marine City, Michigan, but without the stipple paint; oversized with huge keels, rare form which adds to the value. **$300–$400** pair

(*Rear*) Black duck from northern Michigan factory, slightly worn original paint, **$50–$60**. (*Front*) Bluebill drake, maker unknown, Houghton Lake, Michigan, area, **$40–$50**.

Two decoys from Mt. Clemens, Michigan, area: (*Left*) Made by Joe Begin, has unusual sand finish paint, **$70–$80**. (*Right*) Very worn paint but is by known carvers Pecor Fox and Nick Purdo. **$65–$75**

Decoys from Hamilton Bay, Ontario. Most decoys from that area were repainted often, making the repaint quality of some importance. (*Left*) Decoy made by Red Weir, c. 1930, **$125**; (*Right*) Decoy made by Ek Morris displays the unusual drop keel common to the area, **$100**.

Canvasback drake by Ralph Reghi, Detroit, Michigan, 1930s. This decoy has been repainted, but it does have outstanding form and a "name" carver. It would be worth considerably more than **$200–$300** if it were in almost perfect condition.

(*Rear*) Oversize canvasback drake made by Budgeon Sampier, Lake St. Clair. It is hollow with old "working" paint, **$200**. (*Front*) Small bluebill hen, maker unknown, strong paint, Lake Ontario area, **$145**.

(*Front*) Mason Standard Grade glass-eye model, worn original paint with some touch-up, character added by mouse chews on the bill. Example as is, **$100**; if perfect, **$250–$300**. (*Rear*) Unusual turned-head sleeper by Dodge Decoy Factory, Detroit (1884–1894). Many layers of old paint detract from the quality of this example, but the value is enhanced by the age and unique features. **$150** up

Mallard drake from the Mason Decoy Factory of Detroit (1894–1924). The condition of the paint is very important to the value of Mason decoys, as is the physical condition. This one has some of the original paint and is a "premier grade hollow," but has a tail chip not uncommon on this grade of Mason, **$400**. If the decoy were perfect, it would be valued at **$1000** and up.

Ralph Malpage of London, Ontario, made both of these decoys at some point in the 1950s. Both are in original paint, but the wood duck (*front*) was never in the water **$150**. The canvasback has some slight wear from use that adds character to the decoy. **$100**

Canvasback drake made for deepwater shooting by Fern Buck of Michigan. The decoy was used in Lake Erie and has worn and dirty paint, but it is still a classic. **$200** plus

Exceptional hen mallard made by Tom Schroeder (1885–1976) of Fair Haven, Michigan. Fine feather carving and wing detail, classic head, original paint, and a major maker. **$1500** plus

Lake Erie canvasback, probably made by Bill Dalka. The decoy has the brand of his brother, Hy Dalka. The "bobtail" design allowed late-season ice to roll off the back so as not to sink or overturn the decoy. **$100–$200**

Black duck made by Frank Schmidt of Detroit. Excellent carving job with strong paint. Minor damage reduces value to about **$400–$500**.

Canvasback drake made by Billy Quigle and Jack Rufus of New Baltimore, Michigan. Several carvers in the area produced similar decoys, and many of them were hollow. The keel design is also common to the area. This example is solid, c. 1930, and carries its original paint. **$150**

Decoy from Kent County, Ontario, on Lake St. Clair; carver is probably Frank Deroevan, paint is original with especially fine comb painting on the back; unique keel. **$300–$400**

The decoy is having its heavy overpaint gradually chipped away in hopes that the earlier paint underneath may be preserved.

Pair of canvasback decoys with unusual carving under the bills, good "working" repaint, small size; decoys are hollow, and the carver is unknown. **$300–$500** pair

(*Front*) Redhead hen, maker unknown, stylish, perky high head, hollow, very old, good repaint, probably from Harsens Island, Lake St. Clair, **$125–$150**.(*Rear*) Rare metal head decoy, probably from Mt. Clemens, Michigan, and made by Jim Kelson. The weight of the head made keeping these decoys upright in the water a real problem and limited their popularity. **$200–$300**

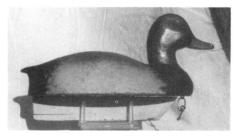

Redhead drake by Paul Fraley, New Baltimore, Michigan, repainted, possibly by the carver. **$50–$75**

Bluebill drake, Irv Malisky, New Baltimore, Michigan, 1920s, original paint, **$125–$150.**

(*Front*) Another excellent decoy, delicate scratch painting, original with beautiful patina, not hollow, 1900 or earlier, **$800**. (*Rear*) Very folksy old bird by "Captain" Meldrum, Harsens Island, good original paint, hollow, **$150–$200**.

Pair of mallards from Port Huron, Michigan, area, maker unknown; value of the pair is in folksiness and would nearly disappear if the paint were not perfect. **$90** plus, pair

Two factory decoys with the maker unknown: (*Front*) Mallard in nearly mint condition, **$75**; (*Rear*) Mallard in its original paint, **$60**.

(*Left*) Coot decoy; similar examples were often used as "confidence" decoys to fool more desirable ducks. This little gem is from Illinois and has its original paint, **$75**. (*Right*) Turnhead pintail drake from California, original paint; these decoys are not real old, but their value has been increasing dramatically as Californians discover their own carvers. **$150–$200**

Canvasback drakes from a rental operation at Saginaw Bay; have taken a beating from heavy use, been repainted many times. **$40** each

This beauty has never been in the water. We don't know who did the carving but initials "M P" on the bottom. Mid-1940s. **$400**

Factory decoys: (*Left*) Repainted bluebill, probably a Victor from Mississippi, sold by the hundreds of thousands. Good examples in strong paint have some value, **$45** up; (*Rear*) Gundlefinger decoys, Jefferson City, Missouri, original paint with a rare factory stamp on the bottom, **$75–$125**.

New carving by Manny Merchant of Marion, South Carolina. Difficult to place a value on. Value is in quality and knowing the carver. **$200–$300**

(*Left*) Folksy bluebill, hollow inletted head, **$150**. (*Rear*) Canvasback drake from Lake Erie, no real pedigree, nice head, bobtail, **$50–80** depending on paint.

A canvasback and a bluebill by H. H. Ackerman of Michigan, very folksy and clunky, value rising on his decoys if paint is good; they are early (pre-1950) and distinctive. **$50–$70**

Bluebill pair by Chris Smith of Algonac, Michigan, founder of Chris Craft Boats; hollow, c. 1900, good working paint and "name" carver. **$400–$500**, pair

Fish decoys used for ice fishing. **$25–$75** each

Seagull decoy, hard to find, used as a "confidence" decoy; this example has original paint and is hollow; 1920s. **$200–$300**

7

COUNTRY
ANTIQUES
AT AUCTION

Copake Country Auctions

Michael Fallon is an auctioneer and appraiser who conducts cataloged Americana auction sales of formal and country furniture, Shaker, quilts, coverlets, hooked rugs, samplers, and folk art. Mr. Fallon's business, Copake Country Auctions, is located at Box H, Copake, New York 12516 (518-329-1142). He is a member of the National Auctioneers Association, New England Appraisers Association, International Society of Appraisers, and the Columbia County Chamber of Commerce.

Copake Country Auctions has a unique commission rate for its cataloged Americana sales: 7 percent commission plus $10 per item. The value listed under each picture is the actual price paid at auction for the item. It does not include the commission fee.

Hudson Valley kas, 1720–1740, original blue painted finish. **$13,000**

Early nineteenth-century Sheraton server. **$1000**

St. Andrews cupboard, French Canadian in origin. **$3500**

Gustav Stickley magazine table. **$1000**

Cherry country Hepplewhite five-drawer chest. **$750**

French Canadian cupboard. **$3800**

Tramp-art sewing table. **$525**

French Canadian cupboard. **$5200**

Matching set of four step-down Windsor chairs. **$1900**

Set of four Shaker Mt. Lebanon chapel chairs. **$2800**

Pair of Shaker chair labels. **$600**

Shaker child's school desk from Mt. Lebanon, New York. **$3000**

Miniature Empire chest, **$2500**. Two-drawer Empire stand, **$375**. Two-drawer Empire "style" stand, c. 1900, **$150**

Decorated eighteenth-century box, originally from France. **$525**

Pennsylvania storage box. **$4000**

Pennsylvania farm table. **$900**

Gustav Stickley chest. **$2200**

Step-back cupboard. **$3500**

Hudson Valley tavern table, 1680–1710. **$4200**

Shaker two-drawer blanket chest. **$2600**

New York state whirligig. **$2900**

Indian whirligig. **$900**

Twentieth-century Uncle Sam. **$300**

Wallace Nutting trademark signature on chair.

Signed Wallace Nutting Windsor chair.
$650

Long Island fence-post head. **$225**

Crandall school figures. **$350**

Painted and decorated game board. **$275**

Nineteenth-century Masonic gate. **$450**

Wooden horse weather vane. **$13,000**

One of a pair of iron gates. **$800** pair

Folksy rocking horse. **$750**

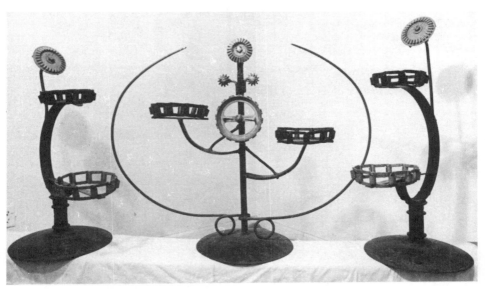

Three-piece plant stand, found in New York state. **$725**

Folk-art boat, 43″ long. **$1485**

Mousetrap. **$475**

Rooster weather vane, L. W. Cushing and Sons. **$4200**

Ethan Allen horse weather vane, 31″ long. **$1600**

Nineteenth-century sandpaper painting. **$500**

English print "Two Hacks," George Stubbs, 1792. **$1100**

Signed E. E. Finch paintings, 1842. **$6250**, pair

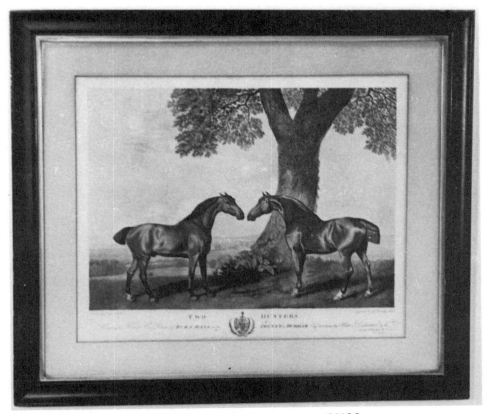

Stipple engraving, "Two Hunters," George Stubbs, 1792. **$1100**

Fraktur from Mt. Pleasant, Pennsylvania.
$4900

New York state pencil drawing "The Homestead," signed "Fritz Vogt." **$1100**

Painting of a side-wheeler, signed "Nemethy." **$500**

Schoolhouse quilt. **$800**

Sunshine and shadows Pennsylvania quilt from Northhampton County. **$500**

Matching pair of quilts, dated 1910. **$2000**, pair

Prices: Looking Back to Look Ahead

To have a better understanding where prices of American country antiques are going, it is necessary to have an appreciation of where they have been. The 50 items below were sold at an auction in Delaware, Ohio, in April 1983. The items described are comparable to many items illustrated and priced for today's market in this book.

CAST-IRON BANKS

1. Indian head, traces of old gold paint, 5″ high: $15
2. Baseball player, worn old red and gold paint, almost 6″ high: $105
3. "Bank" building, worn old dark paint, connecting screw replaced: $10
4. "Mutt and Jeff" old gold paint, approximately 5″ high: $100
5. Elephant on drum, very worn old gold paint, approximately 5″ tall: $17.50
6. Skyscraper "Bank" building, old silver and gold paint, 5″ high: $37.50
7. Globe, worn old red paint, 5¼″ long: $75
8. House, old silver and gold paint with red chimney, approximately 4″ high: $20
9. Boy Scout, very worn old gold paint, almost 6″ tall: $65
10. Seated rabbit, worn old gold paint: $72.50

DECOYS

1. Bluebill drake, primitive working decoy from Flint, Michigan, original paint and glass eyes, c. 1950: $35

2. Primitive Canada goose "sleeper," stylized folk carving with weathered paint and glass eyes, Long Island, 20½" long: $325

3. Canada goose, North Carolina decoy with old worn paint, age cracks in the block and repairs in the neck, approximately 23" long: $225

4. Canvasback drake, primitive working decoy from Saginaw Bay, old worn paint and glass eyes, 16¼" long: $40

5. Bluebill drake, working decoy from Saginaw Bay, old repaint and glass eyes, 13¼" long: $40

TEXTILES

1. Crazy quilt dated 1913, interesting assortment of embroidered fabric with printed ribbons with train fireman memorabilia, "Vivian," "U.S.S. Maine," and various initials, all hand-stitched except for red banding, 54" × 68": $325

2. Two-piece double-weave Jacquard coverlet; blue, red, and white; four rose medallions with bird and house borders and larger corner blocked with "Louicy Long, Fancy Coverlet Wove by J. Heilbronn Ross Co. Ohio 1842," very worn, 72" × 82": $200

3. Two-piece single-weave Jacquard coverlet; red, white, and two shades of blue; corners signed "Wove by D. Smith," edge wear, stains, and a patch, 70" × 88": $150

4. Appliqué quilt, 16 medallions each with 8 stylized tulips in red and ecru, vining border, some stains, 78" square: $325

5. Pieced quilt, bowtie design in multicolored print on white, has wear, 70" × 82": $90

TIN COOKIE CUTTERS

1. Pony, almost 5" long: $77.50
2. Bear cub, 3¼" long: $25

3. Rooster, 4": $55
4. Small dog, 3" long: $32.50
5. Eagle with spread wings, almost 5" wide: $32.50

POTTERY

1. Large yellow ware mixing bowl, tan and white stripes, minor wear, almost 15" diameter, 7" high: $40

2. Yellowware footed salt, white band with brown seaweed decoration, hairlines, 3" diameter and approximately 2" high: $65

3. Yellowware miniature chamber pot, white band with blue seaweed decoration and black stripes, lid repair and hairlines, approximately 2" high: $55

4. Six-gallon stoneware crock; cobalt blue quill work, "6," and simple flourish; small edge chips, mismatched lid, 14" high: $25

5. Stoneware jar, slightly ovoid with brushed cobalt blue floral decoration and wavy lines, decoration is worn, interior lime deposits, 10" high: $80

6. Stoneware crock, impressed mark "Hubbell and Chesebro, Geddes, N.Y."; simple brushed flower and "2" in cobalt blue, surface flakes, 9" high: $65

7. Stoneware crock, impressed mark "J.F. Hart, Ogdensburg," simple brushed flowers in cobalt blue, 9½" high: $95

8. Stoneware jug, light brown Albany slip, lip chips, 12" high: $12.50

9. Yellow ware bowl with brown sponging, minor wear, 7½" diameter and 3½" high: $20

10. Two-gallon stoneware jar with wide mouth; impressed "2" and two splashes of cobalt blue, 10" high: $30

11. Stoneware pitcher, tan glaze, minor rim wear and hairline in base, approximately 11" high: $25

12. Stoneware preserve jar, cobalt stenciled

label "A.P. Donagho, Parkersburg, W. Virginia," good glaze, strong color, 10" high: $65

13. Stoneware jar, stenciled mark "Williams and Reppert, Greensboro, Pa.," brushed cobalt blue lines and "2," some wear, 12" high: $115

14. Four-gallon stoneware crock, brushed cobalt blue "4" with two blue cobalt clouds, minor rim flakes, 12" high: $50

15. Redware pitcher, applied handle and brown speckled glaze, rim and foot repairs, 3½" high: $10

FURNITURE

1. Pair of country Windsor side chairs, bamboo turnings, shaped seats, spindle backs, old and very worn brown repaint with yellow striping and traces of green beneath, 17" seat height: $450, pair

2. One-piece walnut corner cupboard, paneled doors with fully reeded panels, eight panes of glass in each upper door, refinished, edge repairs to doors, base molding and cornice are replaced, 52½" wide and 84½" high: $1350

3. Plank seat side chair with half-spindle back, worn refinishing: $20

4. Country walnut chest, cutout feet and well-scalloped apron, three nailed drawers with beveled overlap and chamfered corners, old refinishing; 45" wide, 19½" deep, and 39" high: $135

5. Poplar rope bed, turned cannonball posts, original rails, refinished and minor age cracks, scalloped headboard: $90

6. Primitive pine schoolmaster's desk, slanted writing surface with narrow shelf beneath, square tapered legs and mortised apron with some old nailed repair, traces of old worn finish; 32" wide, 22" deep, and 34½" high: $25

7. Country stand, square tapered oak legs, dovetailed walnut drawer, mortised walnut apron and one-board poplar top, legs refinished with traces of old white paint, 20¼" × 22" × 23½": $90

8. Poplar pie safe, high square legs and nailed drawer, doors and sides have a total of 12 punched-tin panels with stars and circles: $525

9. Ladderback side chair, 3 slats and turned finials, good old finish and old rush seat, age crack in one slat: $45

10. One-piece poplar wall cupboard, paneled doors, feet have repairs and repairs to cornice, red repaint, 38" wide and 84" high: $300

8

CHRISTMAS COLLECTIBLES

We are often asked for an opinion or prediction about the next American "antique" that collectors will discover, causing prices to escalate rapidly and supplies to diminish. Over the past several years there has been a growing awareness by antiques collectors that some selected collectibles have merit. Mass-produced and marketed Christmas items from the 1930s to 1950s period are starting to gain favor with fans of nineteenth-century Americana, even though it makes these collectors look to the next century.

In the seventh edition of this book we included a chapter that described Christmas-related antiques and their values. In this volume we are providing information and illustrations of the Christmas collectibles that followed Christmas antiques by about two generations. Most were commonly found in chain and local dime and variety stores. At the time these items were initially sold, most people received change from the $1 bill they handed the cashier.

Notes on Christmas Collectibles

- Unlike most antiques, Christmas collectibles are as commonly found in California and Idaho as in Maine and Pennsylvania.
- Flea markets, house sales, resale shops, garage sales, antiques shops and malls are all prime sources for Christmas collectibles.
- At this point condition is a critical factor in the pricing process. If the item is cracked, chipped, discolored, or has a piece missing, it would probably be a good move to find an example in better condition.
- Many mall and collectibles dealers are under the impression that Christmas collectibles only sell from Thanksgiving through December 24 of each year. The rest of the year these dealers tend to store their Christmas items. Make it a point to ask in February or July if a dealer has holidy items for sale.
- The price structure for Christmas collectibles is far from set, and you will find a wide range of prices in different shops and shows for the same item. Keep in mind that most of these Christmas collectibles were produced in fairly large quantities.
- You may be assured that while prices are "reasonable" today, they will not be in several years.

GERMAN GLASS CHRISTMAS ORNAMENTS

$30–$35

$20–$25

$100–$125

$20–$25

$75–$90

$10–$14

$10–$14

$10–$14

$10–$14

$35–$40

$10–$14

Tree, 8″, decorated. **$14**

Decorated 8″ tree with snow. **$12**

Tree, 7″, with battery and light. **$12**

Decorated 8″ white bottle-brush tree. **$12**

White brush tree. **$30**

Music box tree. **$35**

Bottle-brush tree, 15″. **$35–$40**

Gold brush tree, 8″. **$20**

Music box tree, 15". **$45**

Decorated silver metal tree with red beads, 8". **$10**

Bottle-brush tree, 6". **$10**

Wire-brush tree, 8", with original candles. **$75–$85**

Tree with a battery and light, 8″. **$12**

Papier mâché Santa Claus with tree. **$95–$125**

Brush tree with snow decoration, 8″. **$15**

Brush trees ranging in height from 2″ to 8″. **$5–12** each

Bottle-brush tree, 9". **$13**

Early 3½" Santa figure with blue pants, paper, from Japan. **$35**

SANTA CLAUSES

Ceramic Santa. **$20**

Cotton Santa with paper face. **$30**

Cotton Santa with paper face. **$30**

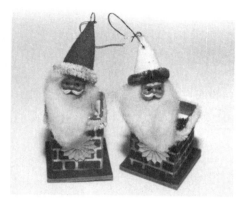

Chimney Santas from Japan. **$20** each

Ceramic Santa from the 1950s. **$10**

Glass Santa ornament. **$75**

Paper figures from Japan. **$15** each

Unusual Santa ornament. **$80**

Cloth and cotton Santa ornament. **$65**

Glass ornament. **$65**

Cotton and cloth figure. **$75**

Plastic figure. **$10**

Sleigh, reindeer, Santa, Mrs. Claus. **$125**

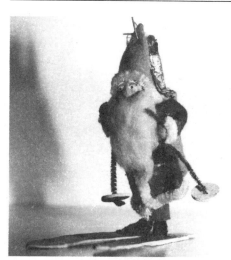

Cloth Santa on skis. **$125**

Cloth Santa figure with base. **$50**

Plastic Santa and sleigh. **$25**

Mask from the 1940s. **$15**

Santa Claus night-light, early 1940s. **$75**

Rubber Santa mask from the 1960s. **$15**

Plastic Santa with bubble light. **$45**

Cast salt Santa and sleigh. **$200**

Cardboard figure from Japan. **$12**

Plastic Santa figures. **$6** each

Plastic Santa and sleigh. **$15**

Plastic Santa ornaments. **$13** each

Plastic Santa with sleigh and pack. **$50**

Santa on reindeer. **$20**

Plastic Santa ornament, 4". **$5**

Plastic Santa, 5". **$15**

Plastic Santa and chimney. **$18**

Plastic Santa with light, 8". **$30**

Plastic Santa and reindeer. **$20**

Plastic Santa in chair, 8″. **$20**

Plastic Santa Claus with light, 8″. **$18**

Plastic Santa, 20″. **$38**

Plastic Santa, 16″. **$50**

Plastic Santa, 15″. **$35**

Plastic Santa, 15″. **$35**

NÖEL ORNAMENTS

Paper candy box, c. 1950. **$12**

Glass ornament. **$35**

Cotton snowman with paper face. **$25**

Glass ornament. **$125**

Plush musical snowman, 18″. **$50**

Mrs. Claus musical doll. **$50**

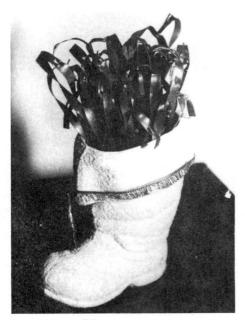

Santa's boot. **$5**

Brush wreath and snowman. **$25**

Plastic snowman and ornaments. **$8**

Kentucky Tavern advertising snowman. **$45**

Plastic church with brush trees. **$25**

Plastic church. **$20**

Plush candy sticks. **$5** each

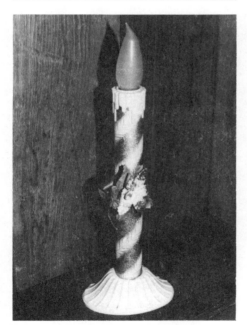

Wax-coated electric candle. **$20**

Plastic snowman, 15". **$20**

Plastic snowman. **$15**

Silver metallic wreath, 12″. **$15**

DECORATED CARDBOARD
HOUSES FROM THE 1930s AND
1940s

$12–$15

$12–15

$12–$15

$12–$15

$10–$12

$10–$12

$35–$40

$15–$20

$15–$20

$35–$40

$30–$35

$35–$45

$30–$35

$12–$18

$15–$18

FINAL
EXAMINATION

The past eight editions of this book have each included a 50-point examination that thousands of people have taken and only a few have passed. Many people have demanded study guides and seminars to assist in prepa-

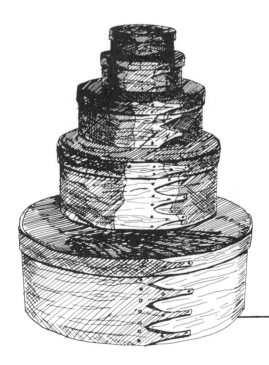

ration for the testing. We have also received telephone calls from four embassies that have requested foreign language versions of the examination.

We are proud to announce that soon editions in Ecuadorian, Etruscan, Ethiopian, and Episcopalian will be in your local bookstores. It is important that you spend as much time with this book as possible. There is a veritable wealth of scholarly information in it, and the majority of it is factual. Like most things in life, you should pick out what best meets your individual needs and pay absolutely no attention to the rest. Generally, we try to test the rest.

We deeply appreciate your positive cards and letters, but threats to do bodily harm to yourself will not result in us supplying the answers to this examination prior to the national testing date. Don't be nervous; failure is a part of life and probably something you have already experienced on a daily basis.

Directions

1. Read each question carefully.
2. Ponder the potential answers. If the correct response does not come immediately to mind, put your feet up, smoke a cigar, or make a sandwich, and go on to the next question.
3. There is *usually* only one correct response to each question.
4. Do not discuss your test results or specific questions with anyone else (aunts excluded) or you will disrupt the sophisticated and costly monitoring procedures that we utilize.
5. Each correct answer is worth one point, except where otherwise noted.

---

1. The wood most commonly found in American country furniture is

   a. pine
   b. cherry
   c. walnut
   d. oak

2. What is an "architectural" cupboard? (4 points)

3. It is not uncommon to find an old piece of country furniture with a newly painted finish. What color is the most probable to be selected to fool a potential customer?

   a. red
   b. yellow
   c. green
   d. blue
   e. all are equally popular

4. Rank the items below from the most expensive (1) to the least expensive (7). (6 points)

   ___red painted pine safe with star tins

   ___butter print with hand-carved geometric design
   ___refinished step-back poplar cupboard with a blind front
   ___refinished staved sugar bucket
   ___three-gallon stoneware crock with a stenciled flower
   ___nine-drawer factory-made spice box with original porcelain pulls and lettering
   ___twelve-tube (2 × 6) candle mold with a strap handle

5. If the bottom of one cupboard is placed with the top of another and sold as an "original," we have an example of a "_____" piece of furniture.

6. Which of the terms below would best describe the pottery on display? (3 points)

"thrown"
molded
c. 1900
redware
stoneware
c. 1840
Rockingham glaze
Albany slip

7. What would be the approximate value
of the three pieces on the top shelf?

   a. $40–$75
   b. $100–$150
   c. $200–$275
   d. more than $350

8. It would have been possible in 1910 to
purchase bowls and pitchers like this
in a department store in Green Bay,
Wisconsin.

   true   false

9. How would you date this chair?

   a. 1725–1800
   b. 1825–1860
   c. 1875–1900
   d. after 1900

10. Which of the terms below accurately
describe this chair?   (4 points)

   banister-back
   Windsor
   ladder-back
   "pieced-out"
   turned posts
   armchair
   loop-back
   continuous arms
   replaced seat

11. The seat of the chair is made of

   a. splint
   b. rush

   c. leather
   d. none of the above

12. The chair has an approximate value of

   a. $150–$175
   b. $200–$275
   c. more than $300

13. The two crocks were used primarily
for

   a. butter
   b. pudding
   c. rum cake
   d. a & b
   e. a & c

14. The jug on page 219 could be described as an "ovoid."

    true   false

15. The jug is worth approximately

    a. $75–$95
    b. $145–$195
    c. $285–$375
    d. more than $400

16. In what state were the crocks produced?

    a. Illinois
    b. Iowa
    c. New Hampshire
    d. Pennsylvania

17. Most sugar buckets have the name of their maker impressed into either the bottom or top.

    true   false

18. Rank the following colors of sugar buckets from the rarest to the most common. (3 points)

brown
blue
white
red
refinished
yellow

19. A sugar bucket with "fingers" was probably made by the Shakers.

    true   false

20. This stack of three sugar buckets in column one will cost you a *minimum* of

    a. $125–$150
    b. $200–$275
    c. $330–$400
    d. $600

21. What is the approximate value of this refinished pie safe?

    a. $200–$300
    b. $400–$575
    c. $700–$850
    d. more than $900

22. If this pie safe had early blue paint, what would be its value?

    a. $200–$300
    b. $400–$575
    c. $700–$850
    d. more than $900

23. How would you date the pie safe?

    a. 1820–1830
    b. 1900–1925
    c. 1870–1890
    d. 1840–1860

24. Does this safe have "bootjack" legs?

    yes   no

25. Most factory-made pie safes were made of _____.   (3 points)

    cherry
    maple
    pine
    walnut
    poplar
    oak
    sycamore

26. The J.P. Coats spool cabinet is made of pine.

    true   false

27. In its current form, it is worth approximately

    a. $150–175
    b. $200–$275
    c. more than $300

28. If it were refinished, it would be worth _____.

29. The spool cabinet dates from about _____.

    a. 1930
    b. 1850
    c. 1875
    d. 1900

30. This is a _____.

31. It was factory made.

    true   false

32. What is the approximate value of this piece with its original finish intact?

    a. $300–$400
    b. $35–$50
    c. $100–$145
    d. $225–$250
    e. more than $400

33. It would date prior to 1860.

    true   false

Optional Bonus Question
(40 points)

Write your answer in a one-thousand-word essay. Responses should be sent to:

Mr. Buster's World of Hair
RR #9
Padua, Illinois 61709

Question: Discuss the evolution of Ameri- can country antiques in relation to inter- national developments in environmental hazards, geopolitical happenstances, and historical accidents. Your answer should in- clude specific references to Red Ryder, George Steele, world peace, and "Chicago- style" hot dogs.

Scoring Scale

45–50 You have joined an exclusive club. For $29.95 we will send you in- formation about the secret hand- shake and the password that will allow you entrance to the semi- annual meetings.

40–44 You have accomplished some- thing that few before you have ever done. Stay home tomorrow and contemplate your success. The next day apply for a job at a local an- tiques mall that needs a security guard or restroom attendant.

35–39 For $19.95 we will send you a home remediation kit and a fac- simile autographed picture of a pie safe.

Answers

1. a
2. a piece that was originally built into the home
3. d
4. 2, 6, 1, 4, 5, 3, 7
5. married
6. molded, c. 1900, stoneware
7. d
8. true
9. b
10. ladder-back, turned posts, replaced seat, armchair
11. rush
12. c
13. e
14. false
15. c
16. d
17. false
18. blue, yellow, red, brown, white, re- finished
19. false
20. c
21. b
22. d
23. c
24. no
25. oak or poplar
26. false
27. b
28. less
29. d
30. butter churn
31. true
32. c
33. false